CARL RUNK'S

COACHING LACROSSE

Strategies, Drills & Plays from an NCAA Tournament Winning Coach's Playbook

New York Chicago San Francisco Lisbon London Madrid Mexico City
Milan New Delhi San Juan Seoul Singapore Sydney Toronto

Library of Congress Cataloging-in-Publication Data

Runk, Carl.
 Carl Runk's coaching lacrosse : strategies, drills & plays from an NCAA
tournament winning coach's playbook / by Carl Runk.
     p.   cm.
   Includes bibliographical references and index.
   ISBN-13 978-0-07-158843-0 (alk. paper)
   ISBN-10   0-07-158843-4 (alk. paper)
   1. Lacrosse—Coaching.   I. Title.   II. Title: Coaching lacrosse.

 GV989.R86   2009
 796.34'7—dc22   2008023358

1 2 3 4 5 6 7 8 9 10 11 12 13 14 15 16 17 18 19 20   DOC/DOC   0 9 8

ISBN   978-0-07-158843-0
MHID   0-07-158843-4

Interior design by Think Design Group

McGraw-Hill books are available at special quantity discounts to use as premiums and sales
promotions or for use in corporate training programs. To contact a representative, please visit the
Contact Us pages at www.mhprofessional.com.

This book is printed on acid-free paper.

To my loving wife, Joan, for her love and belief in me.

Her endless support and encouragement

have been a comfort to me from the beginning.

Contents

Acknowledgments

My family, Keith, Carl, Curt, and Brenda, for their love.

My grandchildren, Maria, Shannon, Allison, Gabriella, Keith, Julianna, Carl, Alexis, and Nicole, for being my second life. Special thanks to Allie for assisting me in this project.

Leo, Willy, Bob, Jim, Tom, Walt, Van, Carol, Lou, Glenn, Bill, Larry, Jerry, and Charlie for their support and coaching advice given unselfishly from the stands through the years.

Tim Mahoney, Joe Ardolino, Jeff Clarke, and Mark Ruess for their never-ending devotion to our program. Their dedication, devotion, loyalty, and trust have been overwhelming.

To my players at the University of Arizona, who believed in a young, aggressive coach.

To all the young men who played at Towson University and were instrumental in the development and respect we have now acquired.

To Jim Saxon, Joe Ferrante, Danny Nolan, Frank Atwood, Mike Grabner, and Jeff Raugh—young men I will always remember.

To Dr. Mike Higgens for always being there when my lack of computer knowledge was so evident.

Introduction

Lacrosse is unique from other sports in the characteristic immediate friendliness and acceptance of all who participate. A lacrosse person can travel to any area of this beautiful country, meet a total stranger, and feel a warmth of acceptance as soon as it is apparent that both individuals have had some sort of involvement with this great game. With this in mind, I have started each chapter with an anecdote from personal experience.

As a sport, lacrosse has grown immensely. The number of participating players is extraordinarily high, and the technique used by these youngsters is better than ever before. Coaches are more learned and able to instruct at a higher level. This, I believe, can be attributed to the advancement of individual and team techniques, along with the game strategies made available to the coaches through local and national clinics. This has not always been the case, though.

I attended my first lacrosse clinic in Long Island, New York, in 1967. It was my first year as the head coach of Towson University, then known as Towson College. The opportunity to get out and meet new coaches in the game appealed very much to me. The clinic, held in a small dining room at a local restaurant, was not too impressive. There were about six rows of chairs and approximately eight chairs per row. Each coach was dressed in either a sport coat or suit, with a tie. Everyone sat at attention in a military manner and displayed a quiet demeanor. After a while, I felt as if I were at a funeral and occasionally would "give my condolences and sympathy" to a participating member. It was, without a doubt, the most boring ordeal I have ever been through. The clinicians were gifted with the ability to put any or all of the coaches present into a deep trance in no time flat—*and they did!*

An old-timer coach asked me to take an oath, before he went to the big lacrosse field in the sky, that if I ever had the opportunity to speak at a clinic, I would do everything possible not to let anyone experience what he had been forced to endure that day. If it sounds a little exaggerated—it isn't. That's how boring it was. Fortunately, I was seated in the last row and in the seat second from last. The last seat was occupied by a handsome, silver-haired gentleman by the name of Roy Simmons, Sr., the father of the very successful longtime Syracuse coach, Roy Simmons, Jr.

Coach Simmons was the head lacrosse coach at Syracuse and was also an assistant football coach. Being the newly appointed football coach at Towson, I had the opportunity to gain a wealth of knowledge about the game of football—and I did. Apparently, Coach Simmons was just as bored as I was and agreed to let me pick his brain.

We sat in the back and exchanged ideas and notes regarding offensive and defensive techniques and schemes. He was very kind and considerate to a young and aspiring coach that day and probably didn't recognize the positive impression he had made. When I arrived back at Towson, my athletic director asked me if I had a good experience at the clinic. Without hesitation, I responded affirmatively: I *had* learned a great deal and definitely would put those lessons to use.

Nomenclature

To establish continuity on both offense and defense, it is important that both sides of the field be identified and structured. This creates a clear and uniform explanation, along with giving an immediate mental picture for better understanding.

As the offensive players are identified by the numbers 1 through 6, the defensive players are also numbered D1 through D6.

The letters surrounding the 6 area, or hole, are defensive positioning points. (The dimensions of the 6 area are approximately five yards by five yards.) During the course of play, the defenseman is asked to play various areas that need to be protected; for example:

- D4 plays the B area when the ball is in the 3 position.
- D1 supports from the X area when the ball is in the 2 position.
- D2 shows support at the A+ position when the ball is in the 5 position.

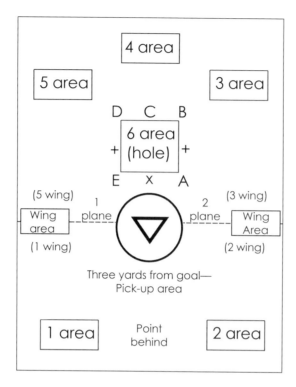

Here is an example of a mental picture:

- No. 24 right—plays 3 position (favorite move)—drives hard to 4 and comes back strong to 3 for sweep shot.
- No. 10 left—1 position—drives point to 1 plane, inside roll for shot.
- No. 15 right—3 position—inverts to 2 position for come-around power shot at 2.

Though no figures have been given, both the offensive and defensive players can get a mental picture of the playing area as well as the tendencies used by the opponents, which better prepares them for the contest and task at hand.

The following key explains the notation used in the figures throughout the book:

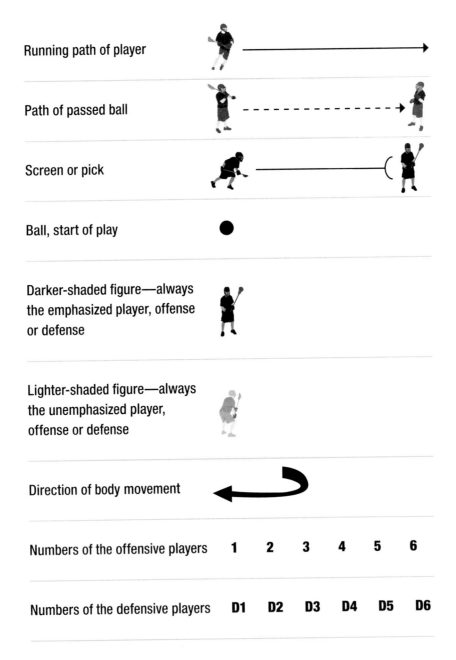

Running path of player

Path of passed ball

Screen or pick

Ball, start of play

Darker-shaded figure—always the emphasized player, offense or defense

Lighter-shaded figure—always the unemphasized player, offense or defense

Direction of body movement

Numbers of the offensive players   1   2   3   4   5   6

Numbers of the defensive players   D1   D2   D3   D4   D5   D6

Offense

IN THE EARLY '70S I WAS FORTUNATE ENOUGH TO BE selected to coach the South Team in the classic North-South seniors lacrosse game held at Cornell University in Ithaca, New York. Dick Edell, then head coach at the U.S. Military Academy, was selected to coach the North. It was a time when this game received tremendous public exposure and was highly popular with the fans.

The night before the big game, the senior players, both North and South, were honored by the city of Ithaca at a downtown evening banquet. Besides the entourage of lacrosse affiliates and officials, the mayor of Ithaca and city council members were also in attendance. After dinner, Richie Moran, longtime successful coach at Cornell University, gathered Dick Edell and myself to a meeting, informing us that we would have to go up on stage and introduce the players of our respective teams. I thought he was kidding, but he was dead serious.

"Richie, you want me to introduce these players, and I don't even know their names!"

"You've got about five minutes to learn 'em," he responded.

I had no idea how I was going to handle this situation and literally hit the panic button. Finally, an assistant coach informed me that I could use the banquet program, which included each player's name, college, and position. Thank the Lord! Here was a solution to a possibly most embarrassing situation. Dick Edell was to go onstage first and introduce his team, which meant at that time, I could study the program and give the impression I knew what the hell I was talking about. With a new surge of confidence, I stood at the base of the stage ready to introduce my team when called on.

In his closing remarks, Edell suddenly paid tribute to the team manager of the North squad, introducing him to the crowd. I wanted to run up onstage and rip his heart out. Everything was going great until he did that. I had about thirty seconds to find out the name of our team manager so I could introduce him after the players. I quickly asked those around me for the name of our manager, but no one knew. As I was introduced and walking up on stage, I passed Edell. He was my last chance.

"Rich, what's the name of my team manager?"

"Oh, your team manager's name is Mel Fernwacker."

"Thanks, buddy, you saved the day."

After introducing my South squad, I announced to the crowd: "I would, at this time, like to introduce you to a young man who for the whole week has helped our squad above and beyond the call of duty. A devoted man who catered to our every need. Ladies and gentlemen, the team manager of the South squad, Mr. Mel Fernwacker. Mel, would you please stand to be recognized!" Everyone in the banquet hall was looking around for Mel, but no one stood up. "Mel, are you out there?"

Finally, a young man in the back stood up and said, "Coach Runk! I went through hell this week trying to get you everything you needed . . . chewing tobacco . . . special drinks . . . setting up the field for your secret practices in the pouring rain . . . and you don't even know my name!"

Well, the crowd laughed unmercifully, and when I looked over to find Rich Edell, he was kneeling on the floor with his head in his hands, covered by a handkerchief and laughing his ass off! For a person who thrives on kidding and fooling people, I have never been so embarrassed in all my life. The big turkey really got me! And I never got the chance to meet Mel Fernwacker!

Basic Principles

Each coach, first and foremost, must take into consideration the offensive potential he has available. There is no reason to employ a system that is unproductive or not conducive to the players' abilities. A common breakdown in coaching is to engage an offense that is destined to miss the mark of success. It may be an offense the coach developed or became interested in at the coach's clinic. But when the offense is used, it doesn't seem to meet the requirements.

Once the season has started, however, the opposing team's *defensive scheme* should dictate the offensive pattern to be used. An example would be an offensive pattern with ball movement from the wing area through the point area being more of a threat than ball movement around the top of the formation. Certain offensive patterns are more appropriate than others against the zone. However, it is not unusual, *on any level*, to see an offensive pattern being applied even when it is not the proper offense to beat the zone. Just because one team has a high percentage with a certain offense does not necessarily mean that another may have the same results.

Years back, I developed a patterned offense that I felt was just what the doctor ordered. I sought out the advice of a peer coach whose team was ranked in the top ten in the country. After explaining and detailing the offense, my friend quickly decided he would adopt it. During the season he would give me feedback on how many goals they scored while using that particular offense. But it was somewhat embarrassing when he asked how the offense worked for our team. Unfortunately, we had very little success with the same offense, so I placed it in the circular file. In essence, I got caught up with an offense that didn't match my personnel.

Soon after, I adopted a policy for matching personnel and offense. Regarding player personnel, a good rule of thumb is to develop strategy based on the following criteria:

- Shooting—both inside and outside
- Stickhandling
- Dodging—can the player penetrate?
- Team quickness
- Team speed

As a matter of proper development with inexperienced players, it would be highly important to teach basic offensive technique and stress the creation of movement via the following:

- **Man with the ball**—if appropriate, go to the goal. If not,
  - Pass and pick for the ball or away.
  - Clear through to the crease looking to screen or pop out.
  - Sluff down, if playing midfield.
- **Adjacent man**—clear through.
  - Screen for the ball.
  - Screen away.
  - Occupy nearest void area.
- **Third man**—attack.
  - See the field.
  - Go toward the ball.
  - Clear through.
  - Fill the vacated area.
- **Midfielder (middie)**—cut to the ball when the far-side attack gets the ball.

Offense comes in many forms. The following are some of the most popular styles being run, along with explanations of the differences and strengths of each.

- Motion offense
- Number series
- Formations

Motion Offense

Cut the Post Down

After a player cuts, he becomes the post man (crease). After the player posts, he drives down and screens for a wing attack on his side.

PHASE 1
- Ball starts at 3.
- 3 passes to 5, who passes to 1.
- As 5 passes to 1, 3 cuts to the ball at 1.

PHASE 2
- If open, 1 feeds 3; if not, he passes back to 5.
- 5 receives the ball and rolls to the outside, coming back to the middle.
- After the cut by 3, 6 backs out toward the sideline away from the ball, and then drives down to screen for 2. 6 then prepares to replace 2 and become the feeder.
- After receiving the ball from 1, 5 then looks diagonally to the mesh between 6 and 2, looking to feed 2 on the quick pop-out.
- If the pop-out is not available, 2 receives the ball and replaces 3 at the 3 position. 2 will pass to 6, who has taken 2's position.
- After 3 cuts, he then becomes the post man (crease) on the opposite side.

Players are now in a position to execute the play from the other side.

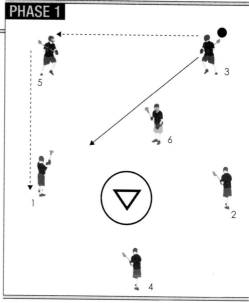

Figure 1.1 Cut the Post Down, Phase 1

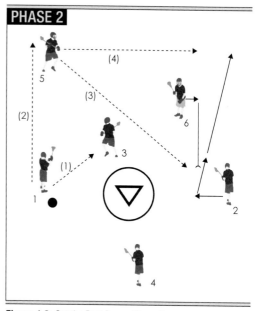

Figure 1.2 Cut the Post Down, Phase 2

PHASE 3

- 5 passes to 2, who passes to 6.
- As 2 passes to 6, 5 cuts to the ball at the 2 position, 6 feeds 5 if open, but if not, 6 passes back to 2. 2 receives the ball and rolls to the outside, coming back to the middle.
- After the cut by 5, 3 backs out toward the sideline away from the ball and then drives down to screen for 1. 3 then prepares to replace 1 and become the feeder.
- After receiving the ball from 6, 2 looks diagonally to the mesh between 3 and 1, looking to feed 1 on the quick pop-out.
- If the pop-out is not available, 1 receives the ball and replaces 5 at the 5 position. 1 will pass to 3, who has taken the 1 position.
- After 5 cuts, he then becomes the post man (crease) on the opposite side.

PHASE 4

The cut-the-post-down offense is a nice change of pace. It should be run full-term before going to the last phase, which is the *short-stick isolation* from point behind.

If 4 does not have the short-stick midfielder, he will exchange positions with whoever does. Assuming 4 has the shorty and is going to attack the right side, all perimeter players will rotate away from the ball in an effort to expose the sliding backup. They should get into a feeding zone and be prepared to receive the ball if the 4 man is unable to penetrate.

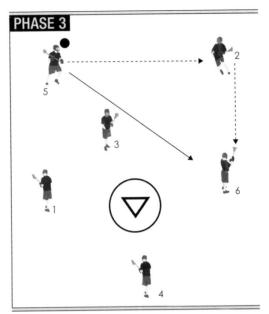

Figure 1.3 Cut the Post Down, Phase 3

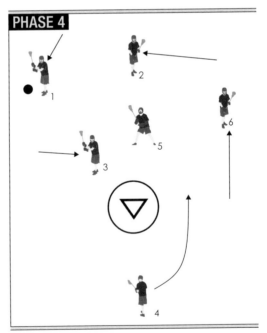

Figure 1.4 Cut the Post Down, Phase 4

Adjustment Call: "Jack"

JACK, PHASE 1

The adjustment called "Jack" can be added anytime while running the cut-the-post-down offense. It is important that all players are aware of the call.

- 3 makes the call, and on his cut toward 1, 3 "jacks" (picks) for 6.
- 6 should pop out to the ball, expecting the feed from 1.

JACK, PHASE 2

If the Jack is not there:

- 1 quickly moves the ball to point behind (4), who in turn passes to 2.
- As 4 passes to 2, 3 screens again for 6.
- If 6 is not available, 2 feeds the ball to 5 for the quick iso at the 4 position.

This completes the Jack call.

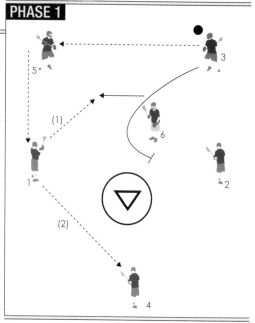

Figure 1.5 Jack, Phase 1

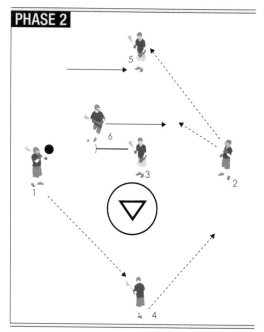

Figure 1.6 Jack, Phase 2

2-2-2 Spoke Offense

The spoke offense is an excellent control-type offense. It is easy to teach and can be used both in the control and scoring modes. When teaching this pattern, the general rules are as follows:

PHASE 1

- **Midfielder with the ball**—If the situation calls for a power sweep (front) or rollback sweep (back door), this player should take advantage of the situation. The second option would be to give the ball to the pop-out middie, 4; the third option is to feed the pop-out attack, his side.

    Anytime a middie gives up the ball, he should exchange with the middie on the crease. The adjacent attackman without the ball, 2, should be alert to give the impression he is exchanging with the high-post man on the crease and continue to scrap across the crease looking for a feed from the attackman, 1.

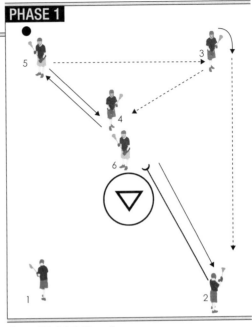

PHASE 1

Figure 1.7 2-2-2, Phase 1

PHASE 2

- **5, middie without the ball**—This player should be concerned with ball movement and exchange with the high-post middie, 4, keeping in mind that this is a definite "pick" move. If the ball is thrown to the diagonal attackman, this player should be prepared to completely cut through, looking for the feed.
- **4, high-post middie**—This player follows the ball movement. He should be ready to pop out when the offside middie is cutting in. If the pop-out is unavailable, he should continue to an up-top position.
- **Attack with ball**—On receiving the ball, this players always looks to feed. If the feed is not there, he passes the ball to the offside attackman or onside middie, and picks and exchanges with the crease.
- **Offside attack**—This player reads the situation. If the ball is carried upfield, he moves over and supports the point position; otherwise, he picks and exchanges with the crease.
- **Crease attack**—Anytime the attack receives the ball, the pop-out is available for the low-post crease. If not, he exchanges with the crease.

Basically, the spoke offense is two separate triangles with multiple exchanges.

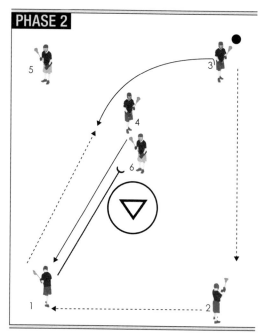

Figure 1.8 2-2-2, Phase 2

1-3-2 Spoke Offense

All responsibilities are the same as in the 2-2-2 formation with the exception of the attack, which is open, having the 6 man behind. Instead of the exchange taking place on the crease, it takes place on the perimeter. The feed occurs at point behind and usually to the middie away from the rotation. This formation affords more individual isolation if needed.

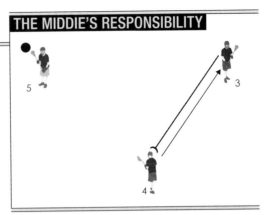

Figure 1.9 1-3-2 Spoke Offense

Figure 1.10 1-3-2 Spoke Offense

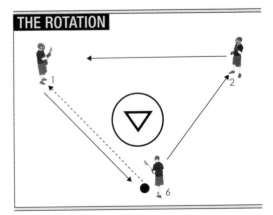

Figure 1.11 1-3-2 Spoke Offense

Wheel Offense

A very popular offense used at various levels is the wheel offense. Many coaches look for constant movement with the intention of catching the opponent off guard and being in a position to take advantage of the situation. This particular offense can contribute to that philosophy.

RESPONSIBILITIES AND RULES

- The 4 position and the point-behind position must always be occupied!
- The player adjacent to the ball must clear through looking to:
  - Pick
  - Curl or fishhook
  - Look for a dump pass
- The second player from the ball should fill the vacated position or look to receive the ball if the penetration move is unavailable.
- The player on the crease should move away from the ball, being ready to receive the ball if an iso attempt is unavailable.

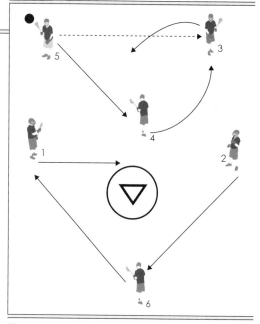

Figure 1.12 Wheel Offense

Look at Figures 1.13 and 1.14 respectively to see the wheel offense illustrated from behind and with the ball at the wing.

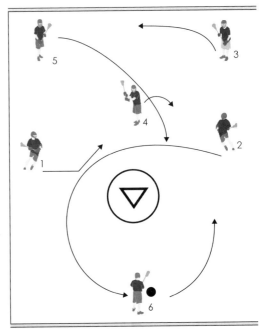

Figure 1.13 Wheel Offense

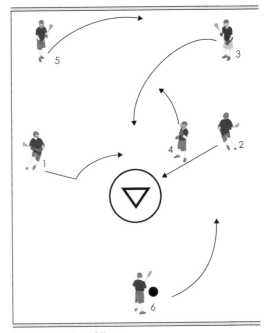

Figure 1.14 Wheel Offense

Number Series Offense

A simple strategy taken from football philosophy and applied successfully to lacrosse was the number series. This series involves certain given plays run within certain categories. Once the players understand the significance of each category, the response becomes highly productive. Using the series, a coach can take his team into a contest feeling confident and assured he is prepared for every situation. The following is an explanation of the series and the possibilities within each area:

- 10 series—isolation matchup series
- 20 series—six-man inbound plays
- 30 series—three-man attack plays
- 40 series—four-man inbound plays
- 50 series—six-man iso and games
- 60 series—six-man offense
- 70 series—three-man midfield plays
- 80 series—zone offense
- 90 series—special situation plays

This offense has many advantages, and it is important that the players believe *they have an advantage* and can be successful within this scheme. A primary concern in adopting this offense is, "Isn't it a great deal to learn?"

In the past and present, football has run the series-style offense very successfully. The players are asked to retain a great deal of offense. In lacrosse, it may seem like a lot for players to remember, but when explained, demonstrated, and executed in a slow, deliberate fashion, the series can be exciting.

First and foremost, the players must be introduced to each phase and how it is applied during the course of the game. They must have a thorough understanding of the advantage of each series. Then this style of play will be more readily accepted.

10 Series

The 10 series is basically the offensive matchup series. It can be applied anytime during the contest when there is a definite mismatch in personnel. The numbers 0 to 5 indicate the position of the isolation, with 0 representing point behind, 1 and 2 representing the wing area, and 3, 4, and 5 designating the top.

A code word alerts players of the desired play. The number of the selected player is given next, followed by the number of the position. An example is "Mary—15—at 4." At this time, whoever is covered by 15 moves to the 4 position and executes the isolation. Obviously, the other players need to occupy their defenders through movement and by exchanging positions.

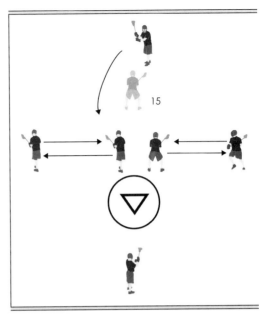

Figure 1.15 10 Series

2-2-2 Formation

The 10 series can also be accomplished by a set pattern. This alternative—and how it is to be performed—is decided by the coaching staff beforehand. The 2-2-2 formation has been used successfully and is a high-percentage isolation move.

RESPONSIBILITIES

- **5, "Mary" man**—Takes a position at the 5 area, passes the ball to the 6 man, breaking out from the crease. 5 then travels to the 4 position directly in front of the goal. 5 must be ready to receive the ball and force to the goal.

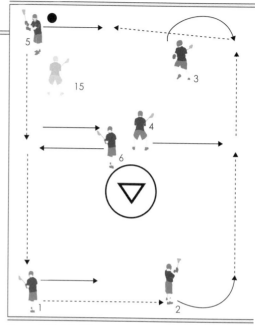

Figure 1.16 2-2-2 Formation

- **6, crease man**—Starts out on the crease and breaks out to the 1 plane to receive the ball from the Mary man. 6 quickly relays the ball to 1 and returns to the farside crease area on the goal. 6 prepares for a possible feed from 5 if the slide takes place.
- **1**—After receiving the ball from 6, 1 runs to point behind and then passes to 2. 1 will be the backup or the sneak for 5.
- **2**—Receives the ball from 1, and then runs out toward the side restraining line before passing to 4. 2 stays there and watches the development.
- **4**—Starts on the crease and moves toward the restraining line when 1 gets the ball. 4 will take the ball from 2 and quickly pass up to 3.
- **3**—Begins in the normal 3 position and moves out toward the side restraining line when 1 throws to 2. Upon receiving the ball from 4, 3 must quickly drill the ball to 5.

In essence, the formation starts in a basic 2–2–2 and through movement, reestablishes the same formation, but one position over to the left. The setup applies stress to the defense because they are disciplined to follow their man. They are placed in a weakened backup position. Quick passing, especially as the ball turns the corner at the 4 position, is the order of the day.

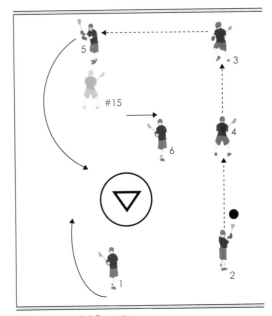

Figure 1.17 2-2-2 Formation

20 Series

This series is a six-man inbounds format. Anytime the ball should go out of bounds, it is in the best interest of the offensive group to reorganize and take advantage of the situation. Unless you have an outstanding player—and that's questionable—freelancing doesn't cut it. A team must always be prepared, in all situations, to be a positive force. The 20 series gives just that support. A few examples of this series follow.

20

On the given call, the ball can be brought in by either attackman, with 1 setting up the play.

RESPONSIBILITIES

- **1**—Shows a power move by coming around, dropping off, and passing to 5.
- **4**—Starts to cut to 1; then hesitates outside and diagonally away from 6, patiently waiting for 5 to pass the ball to 3.
- **2**—Waits for the preceding moves to happen; then moves to the crease, setting up a screen for 4, who runs an undercurl off the double screen, preparing to receive the ball from 3. 4 is now in a good position to take the shot.

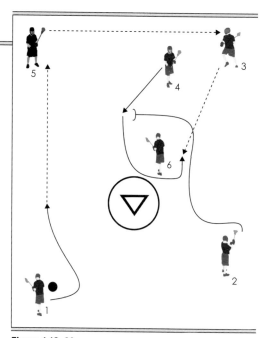

Figure 1.18 20

22

This basically is run out of the 1-4-1 formation.

RESPONSIBILITIES

- **5**—Starts out at the 4 position. When 1 gets the ball, 5 softly cuts toward 1 and sets up above 6, approximately four yards. He stays in this position until 2 powers to the right and passes to 3. At this time, 5 cuts diagonally toward 2.
- **1**—Plays out on the 1 wing position, and on receiving the ball from 2, passes it right back to 2. At this time, 1 moves behind, while watching the ball, up to the 5 position as a backup or safety.
- **2**—Brings the ball in bounds, passes to 1, and waits for the return pass from 1. He then powers to the right and passes to 3.
- **4**—Plays a high crease approximately three to four yards diagonally up from 6 and five yards away. As 2 passes to 3, 5 cuts to the ball. 4 cuts right off of 5's hip and screens for 6.
- **6**—After the X cut by 5 and 4, 6 waits for the screen and cuts toward the ball. He should be prepared to stop, plant, and take a hard shot on the goal. It will be there!
- **3**—Plays a high wing position, waits for the play to develop, and on receiving the ball, should be prepared to feed 6 on his cut.

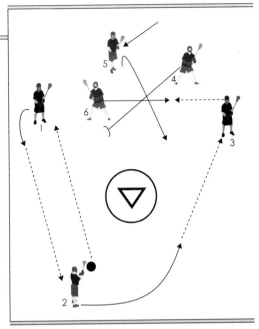

Figure 1.19 22

COACHING POINT *The timing between 4 and 5 is highly important. 4 must cut right off of 5's hip.*

30 Series

The 30 series is strictly an attack series. It can be used while the ball is in play or during a dead ball situation. When calling this series, it is important to signal the midfield that the attack is preparing to execute a play. This can be done by simply giving the "Spread out, middies!" call, which alerts the midfield to keep their defenders busy and out of the way of the attack.

30 Post

RESPONSIBILITIES

- **1**—Makes the call and brings the ball in play. 1 drives hard to the goal and looks to feed the scrape man, 6.
- **2**—Must be alert and read 1. When 1 starts his move, 2 drives down to the onside, looking like he is cutting to the ball but actually moving into a good screening position.
- **6**—Plays off the crease approximately three yards, and is looking to scrape off of the screen by 2. At this time, 6 prepares for the feed.

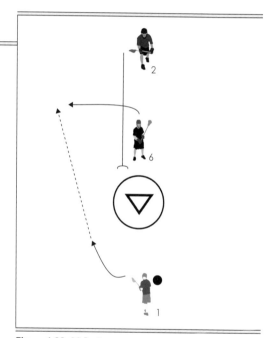

Figure 1.20 30 Post

30 Bump

An old basketball screen-and-roll move, the bump is a high-percentage play in lacrosse. The objective is to show the screen, allowing the covering defender to give the switch call. At this point, D6 switches coverage to 2 and D2 is responsible for 6. However, D2 is now out of position, which is a definite advantage for the offense.

RESPONSIBILITIES

It should be pointed out beforehand what side the play is to be run. In Figure 1.21, the 1 man is going to his right.

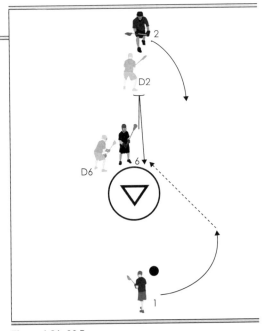

Figure 1.21 30 Bump

- **1**—Brings the ball into play, drives hard to the right, and looks to feed the primary cutter, 6; the secondary feed would be 2 on the back door.
- **2**—Reads the direction of 1 and cuts wide, away from the ball, allowing the defense to make an easy switch. 2 should be available to receive the ball on the backdoor cut if the primary feed is not there.
- **6**—As soon as the 1 man gives the read, 6 turns and screens the defender covering. Immediately after 2 cuts away, 6 pushes off the defender while drop stepping with the onside foot and turns, creating a cushion between himself and the defender. He then drives to the onside goal, looking for the quick feed.

30 Scrape

Almost the same move and application as the bump, only with the 6 and 2 men playing a double crease.

RESPONSIBILITIES

- **1**—Brings the ball into play, drives hard to the right, and looks to feed the primary cutter, 2; the secondary feed would be 6 on the high scrape.
- **2**—As soon as the 1 man gives the read, 2 turns and screens the defender covering 6. As soon as 6 cuts away, 2 pushes off the defender while drop stepping with the onside foot; 2 turns, creating a cushion between himself and the defender; and drives to the onside goal, looking for the quick feed.
- **6**—Reads the direction of 1 and cuts high, away from the ball, allowing the defense to make an easy switch. 6 is available to receive the ball if the primary feed is not there.

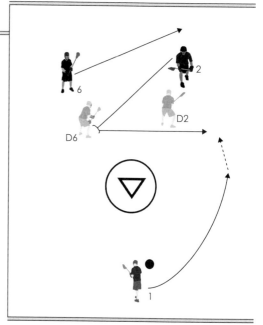

Figure 1.22 30 Scrape

40 Series

The 40 series is quite similar to the 30 series with one exception, the 4 man. This is an exciting four-man offensive set involving the 4 man with entire attack. A "spread out" call alerts the up-top middies, both 3 and 5, to occupy their man and stay away from the crease. This is a quick-hitter-type offense. If it's successful . . . great! If not, just move on.

The following setups have been used with a great deal of success:

40 Scrape (Screen the Screen)

RESPONSIBILITIES

- **2**—Brings ball in bounds, and starts his move to the right to set up the first screen. Reverses direction, and prepares to feed 4 on the second screen.
- **6**—Sets up three yards from the crease and is ready to cut hard to the outside after the screen, calling for the ball to attract attention.
- **4**—Should be a good "finisher," positioned on the outside left of the three-man crease. As the attackman brings the ball to 4's side, 4 drives in quickly to screen for 6, and then hesitates and waits for the screen by 1. 4 cuts off of the screen, looking for the ball on a feed from 2.
- **1**—Positioned on the outside right of the three-man crease. As soon as 6 cuts to the offside, 1 screens for 4. Timing is highly important in this move.

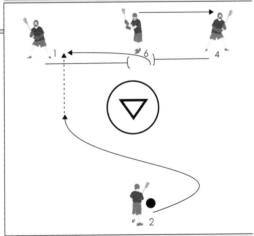

Figure 1.23 40 Scrape (Screen the Screen)

42 Back Door

RESPONSIBILITIES

- **2**—Brings ball in from out of bounds and passes to 1 as he drops off the crease to receive the ball. 2 then runs to a spot on the off-center crease and post.
- **1**—Positions to the offside crease, and on the whistle, drops down toward the back line, receiving the ball from 2. After 2 has set up the post, 1 drives hard across the screen on a come-around. At this time, he is completely aware of 4 on the backdoor cut and feeds to a high stick.
- **6**—Takes a stationary position about five yards above the crease and reads the progress of the play.
- **4**—Plays approximately three yards above 6 in a diagonal position. He always plays on the ball side and must read his defender. As 1 is coming around, 4 must wait for the defender to turn toward the ball. At that time, 4 cuts to the back door, looking for the quick hitter.
- **3 and 5**—Abide by the "spread out" call.

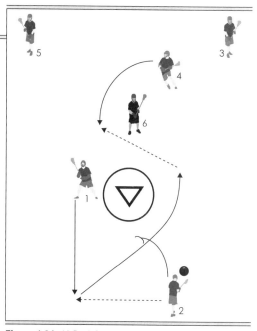

Figure 1.24 42 Back Door

50 Series

One of the most popular formations used in the game presently is the 1-4-1. This formation can be applied at any position, particularly the 4 and point positions, as well as from the side, the 1 plane and 2 plane. As an iso formation, it can also be used as a decoy to draw the slide and dump the ball off.

50 Dump

RESPONSIBILITIES

- **4**—Starts with the ball in the 4 position up top, moves slightly to the left and comes back hard right, giving the impression of a threat, and tries to draw the slide. He then passes the ball to 1 on the curl and supports the play.
- **5**—Plays the outside position of the 1-4-1 formation. As 4 changes direction, 5 screens immediately for 1.
- **1**—Stationed inside of 5, 1 curls outside on 5's screen, looking to receive the ball. As 1 receives the pass from 4, 1 has three options: (a) take the shot, (b) feed 3 on the quick pop-out, or (c) pass the ball to 2 at the point.
- **6**—Reads the play of 4, hesitates, and when the pass is made to 1, screens for 3.
- **3**—Is in the outside wing position, away from the ball. As the play develops, 3 waits for the screen by 6 and comes off the screen quickly and in a position to shoot the ball.

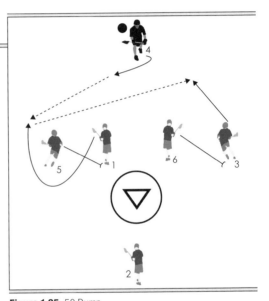

Figure 1.25 50 Dump

52 Mike

This is run out of the 1-4-1 formation.

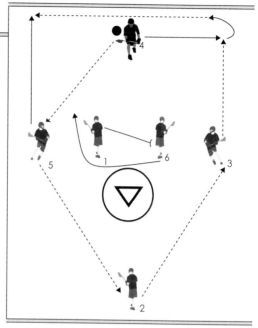

Figure 1.26 52 Mike

RESPONSIBILITIES

- **4**—After moving the ball around the field one time, 4 passes the ball to the "Mike" middie (isolator) and rotates to the 3 position. He then prepares to quickly pass the ball again to the mike middie (5), who has rotated up to the 5 position (if he is a left-hander) or the 4 position (if he is a right-hander).
- **5**—Stationed at the outside 1 wing position. After 5 passes the ball to 2 at point behind, he prepares to take a position up top, for the iso, at either the 5 or 4 position, wherever he feels confident. After receiving the ball from 4, 5 quickly drives to the cage for the shot.

    Option 2: look for the pop-out by 6.

- **1**—Positioned at the left side of the crease, 1 screens for 6 on the iso move by 5.
- **6**—Positioned at the right side of the crease. On the iso move by 4, 6 must be alert to undercut off the screen by 1.

53 Wings

As discussed earlier, the 50 series can be run from the top position, point position, and the wing position very effectively. The formation usually stays the same unless another is desired. The following formation is an example of the 50 series attempted from the 1 plane (wing).

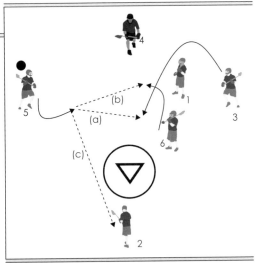

Figure 1.27 53 Wings

RESPONSIBILITIES

- **5**—Starts the play at an isolated 1 plane position. 5 diagonally takes a few steps to his right and quickly split-dodges to his left. This is the key for the others to initiate their movement. 5 then looks to (a) feed 3, (b) feed 6, or (c) pass the ball to 2 at the point position.
- **3**—Plays at a 2 plane position, and slowly slides in about five yards away from 6 and 1. On 5's cue, 3 scrapes across the top and rolls down toward the goal looking for the feed.
- **6**—Begins at the low-post position on the offside of the crease. His read is 3's cut. 6 pops out diagonally, looking for the feed.
- **1**—Plays a high-post position above 6. 1 must be available to receive the ball on a pass to 2.

60 Series

Basically, this category is the wide-open series—open for various formations and play. It serves to execute plays from the basic to the extreme offense.

60 Regular Behind, Phase 1

The 1-3-2 is an example of initiating the 60 series from a basic formation and moving to a more complex 1-4-1 formation.

RESPONSIBILITIES

- **3**—After passing to 5, 3 times his cut and scrapes off of 4, looking for the feed from 1. If the feed is not there, 3 will wait for the screen by 4. This should take place when 2 receives the ball. At this time, he again cuts to the ball.
- **5**—Passes the ball to 1 and then rotates up to the 4 position, getting ready for the iso up top.
- **1**—On receiving the ball, 1 looks to feed 3 scraping across 4. If the feed is not there, 1 passes the ball to 6 at point behind.
- **2**—Receives the ball from 6 and looks to the crease to feed 3. If 3 is not open, 2 moves the ball up to 5 for the top isolation.
- **4**—Plays a high-crease position, visually following the ball. As 2 receives the ball, 4 screens for 3.
- **6**—At point behind, 6 assists in moving the ball around the horn.

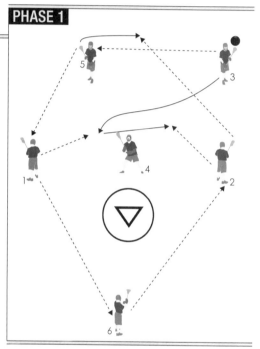

PHASE 1

Figure 1.28 60 Regular Behind, Phase 1

60 Regular, Phase 2

RESPONSIBILITIES

- **5**—On receiving the ball from 2, 5 prepares to go into the isolation mode. Assuming he is going to his right, he drives slightly to the left and comes back hard to the stick side to take the shot (1). If this option isn't available, 5 looks to pass the ball to 4 on the loop (2). He then returns to the 5 position, ready to run the exact play to the opposite side.
- **1**—From an outside position, 1 reads 5's move and comes in to down screen for 4. 1 reads the situation and returns to his outside position.
- **4**—In the inside left crease position, 4 watches 5 and waits for the screen by 1. On the loop, he looks for the quick hitter (quick stick shot). If it is not there, 4 pushes the ball to the point to 6. He then reads the play and returns to the high-crease position, ready to run the offense to the other side.
- **6**—Is ready to back up the shot by 4. If the shot is not there, 6 waits to receive the ball from 4. At this time, he quickly forces to the right, looking to feed 3 on the pop-out. After giving the ball to 3, he resettles at the point position ready for the second half.
- **2**—As 6 forces to his side, 2 quickly down screens for 3 on the pop-out.
- **3**—Executes a quick pop-out to his side. If the shot is not there, 3 rolls to the outside toward the 3 position, where he passes the ball to 5, which starts the offense at the opposite side.

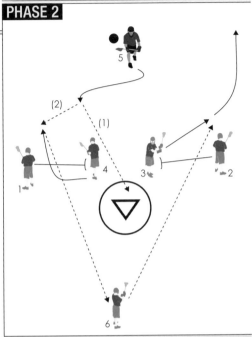

Figure 1.29 60 Regular, Phase 2

70 Series: Midfield Series

There are times during the game when it would be appropriate for the midfield to put the ball into play without the inclusion of the attack. The 70 series gives the group that opportunity. As soon as it is called, the other players understand that they are to occupy their defenders, keeping them away from the play. At this time, the midfielders can select and do their own thing.

70

RESPONSIBILITIES
- **4**—Starts with the ball at the 4 position. Passes to 5 and picks away at 3.
- **3**—Begins by going upfield a few yards and then turns and cuts off the screen, looking for the ball.
- **5**—After receiving the ball from 4, 5 takes a few steps toward the end line, comes back, and passes the ball to 3.

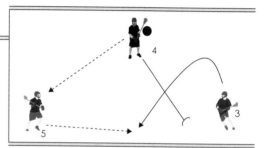

Figure 1.30 70

72

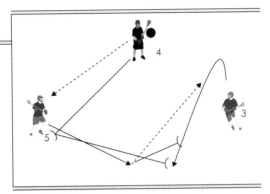

Figure 1.31 72

RESPONSIBILITIES

- **4**—Starts with the ball and passes to 5; then picks for 5. After the pick, he turns and follows 5 for the double offset screen for 3.
- **5**—After receiving the ball from 4, 5 starts toward the center, feeds the ball to 3, and then sets up a screen for 3.
- **3**—Curls upfield, awaiting the feed from 5. Once he receives the ball, he drives off the double screen toward the goal, looking to shoot the ball.

74

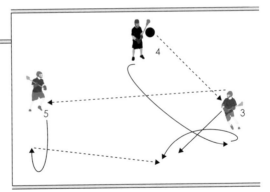

Figure 1.32 74

RESPONSIBILITIES

- **4**—Passes the ball to 3, and then clears through to the 3 position. Hesitates until 5 is available to feed 4 on the scrape off of 3.
- **3**—Receives the ball from 4, quickly passes to 5, and then takes a position toward the middle and five yards diagonally from 4.
- **5**—After receiving the ball from 3, 5 drives down toward the backline for timing purposes only. When 5 rolls back, 4 starts his move off the screen toward the goal. 5 looks to feed 4.

75 Shorty

- The 75 (shorty) is a three-man exchange up top and needs the support of the 6 man on the crease. He must recognize what is taking place and support the game. Two middies, depending on the iso, will drop to the crease, one on each side of the 6 man. As the iso is approaching, one middie will down screen, while the other loops out to get the ball.

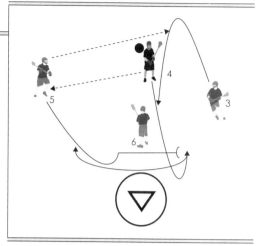

Figure 1.33 75 Shorty

RESPONSIBILITIES

- **4**—Initiates the play by passing to 5. 4 then drops to the crease alongside the 6 man. When the iso man is starting to drive to the cage, 4 waits for the screen by 5, loops off to the outside, and waits for the feed from 3.
- **5**—After receiving the ball from 4, 5 passes to 3, who is breaking high to receive the ball up top the 4 position. 5 then drops down to the crease, opposite 4, and will screen for 4 at the appropriate time.
- **3**—As the play develops, 3 should break to the top of the 4 position, ready to receive the ball. When 3 does, he breaks hard to the cage on an iso move. If the shot is available, he takes it. If not, he looks for the loop by 4 and feeds him.

Though there are many schemes to be run, these four, when drilled properly, have been run with success.

80 Series: Zone Offense

The 80 series is a format that all teams should have available during the course of the season. It is the zone series. How often, on any level of play, have we watched teams apply a form of the zone, with the offensive group unaware as to what to do? Unfortunately, the adjustment is usually ineffective. It is the coach's responsibility to be prepared for any situation. To have the attitude that it will not happen could be detrimental to the team's success. The 80 series will keep a team somewhat prepared for just that kind of a situation. I am always

amused at the scenario of a zone suddenly being applied, the players yelling to the coach, "They're running a zone!" and the coach with outstretched arms, palms up, seeming to say, "What the hell do you want me to do?"

Competing Against the Zone: Basic Principles

- Understand the zone being applied.
- Choose the proper formations.
- Use screens properly.
- Have confidence.

Understand the zone being applied. One of the primary instruments in contesting a zone is having a basic knowledge of how that particular zone operates. If a coach has an understanding of each defensive player's responsibilities within the scheme, his chances of being successful with the offense increase. It is important to know the backers and where they come from: Does the crease defender have one-on-one responsibilities? Is it a matchup-type zone (with adjacent slides)? Or is it a "black zone" (the double backer), with the slides basically coming from the crease or D4 position? There are a number of variations, and the more familiar a coach is with the zone that's being applied, the more successful he can be in attacking that particular defensive scheme.

Choose the proper formations. When competing against a zone, I have found that being in the proper formation is of utmost importance. The following are a few formations that cause havoc to zone defenses: 2-2-2 formation with carries, fills, and movement; 3-3 formation with front screens; 1-4-1 formation with carries, fills, and screens; and, last but not least, the 2-4 formation, with two players behind the goal and four across the front, approximately 5 to 7 yards upfield.

Use screens properly. Screens can be extremely important against the zone and can be directed to either the outside or the inside cuts.

Have confidence. The confidence level of the offensive group becomes extremely high when the offensive zone segment is practiced in the daily schedule. The youngsters should be aware of what to do and, more important, why they are doing it. A coach will derive tremendous pleasure and satisfaction in watching his offensive group adjust immediately to the defensive change on the field. At this time, the mental-edge advantage can be overwhelming.

COACHING POINT *Since the defense is at its **strongest** when the ball is out **front**, there is no reason to constantly pass the ball around the front perimeter. It would be to the advantage of the offensive team to **work the ball around the wings and behind**, since this is where the zone usually weakens. When the ball turns the corner and goes behind, the defense must make critical adjustments. At this time, an alert offense can be productive.*

82 Swing, Phase 1

Out of the 2-2-2 formation, assuming all offensive corners are covered by defensive corners D1, D2, D3, and D5, the ball starts at the 3 position by 3.

RESPONSIBILITIES

- **3**—Passes to 5 and follows his pass to the 5 position and down toward the back line approximately five to seven yards. At this time, 3 is about five yards above 5.
- **5**—Receives the ball from 3 and forwards it to 1. 5 then follows the pass approximately ten yards.
- **1**—Hesitates after receiving the ball from 5, which forces D1 to play him. After passing to 2, 1 follows his pass to the offside crease area, not point behind, and waits for the return pass from 2.
- **2**—After receiving the ball from 1, 2 draws D2 and takes him to the plane, turns, and passes the ball back to 1 at the offside crease area.
- **6**—Positioned five yards up and to the same side as 2. When 2 passes to 1, he will drive hard to that side of the crease, mainly to draw coverage by D6.
- **4**—Positioned on the double crease, same side as 1. As 2 overloads and passes the ball back to 1, 4 should be taking a position diagonally off the crease, behind at the 1 position.

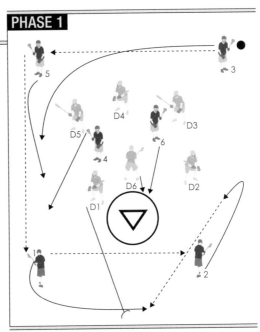

Figure 1.34 82 Swing, Phase 1

82 Swing, Phase 2

RESPONSIBILITIES

- **1**—Received the ball from 2 off center. He draws D1 from his position to cover him. 1 then passes the ball to 4, who has replaced him at the 1 position.
- **4**—Must be alert that he could be open if D5 doesn't slide down to play him. If he is, he quickly goes to the cage for the shot. His primary responsibility is to look at 5 cutting to the cage or at 3 for the easy shot. 4 should be covered by D5, which means D4 will be responsible for 5 on the drive to the cage and also 3 on the outside shot. There is no need to be concerned with D3 as he is conditioned to stay on his side.
- **5**—As 4 receives the ball, 5 cuts to the cage with his stick held high, waiting for the high feed. If D4 does not respond to 5, he should be open.
- **3**—Plays about five yards above 5 and should be ready for the quick, hard bounce shot.
- **6**—When 1 receives the ball, 6 breaks hard for the offside crease. This move will draw D6 to cover him.

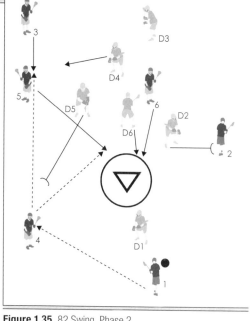

PHASE 2

Figure 1.35 82 Swing, Phase 2

COACHING POINT *The second time "82 swing" is called, add the word "Jack," which simply means 5 will look to screen D4, giving 3 the open shot. This is sometimes referred to as "legal cheating."*

84 Curls

Very similar to 82 swing, but instead of 1 going to the offside crease behind, he goes toward the back line to receive the pass from 2. This will attract D1 off the pipe and hopefully cover 1 by the back line.

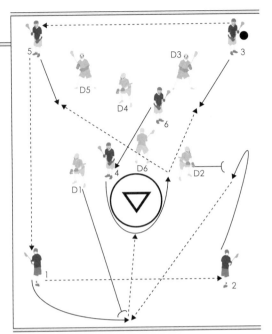

Figure 1.36 84 Curls

RESPONSIBILITIES

- **3**—Starts with the ball and passes to 5, who passes to 1.
- **2**—On the call, 2 carries the ball to the wing area, drawing D2 out to cover him. He turns quickly to pass the ball to 1 by the end line.
- **1**—After passing to 2, 1 takes a position by the end line, behind the crease. When getting the ball from 2, 1 quickly feeds 4, who is curling around the crease.
- **4**—Plays on the crease to the 1 position side. As soon as 1 receives the ball at the back line, 4 runs a quick curl around the crease, receives the ball from 1 and (a) takes the shot, (b) feeds 6 on the back door, or (c) feeds either 3 or 5 in the passing lanes.
- **6**—Plays a high double crease, and must be alert to go to the offside crease (back door).
- **3** and **5**—As the transaction takes place behind them, both must drop down into passing lanes.

85 Uptown

This is a good pattern run out of the 1-4-1 formation. It can be very effective, and it is important to place select players at certain positions. That said, I acknowledge it's difficult to follow at first. But don't be discouraged; once the pattern is worked through, it is quite simple to employ.

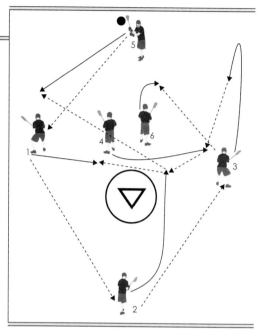

Figure 1.37 85 Uptown

RESPONSIBILITIES

- **5**—Starts the ball movement to his right. After he gives up the ball, he will follow and get himself in a good feeding lane. He easily could be the final shooter.
- **1**—Receives the ball from 5, passes it on to 2 at the point, and goes to the offside crease area, looking for the cross crease feed.
- **2**—Moves the ball up to 3, and follows slowly, waiting to see the development. 2 should be at the goal line extended (GLE) when 4 receives the ball. If 2 receives the ball from 4, he (a) takes the shot, (b) feeds across the crease to 1, or (c) finds and feeds 5 in the passing lane.
- **3**—After receiving the ball from 2, 3 carries the ball to the 3 position, pulling the close defender with him, and then turns and passes to the loop man, 4.
- **4**—Plays an offside high crease. He replaces 3 at the wing position and waits for the pass from 3. His options are to take the shot if it's available, feed the 6 man if he is open, or quickly feed 2 on the come-around.
- **6**—Plays next to 4 on the crease. When 3 carries to the 3 position and passes to 4, 6 should take a few steps diagonally upfield, drawing the crease defender, and expect the feed if he is open.

80 Quick Hitters

This type of offense is used in short time periods, dead ball situations, or as an adjustment to determine exactly what kind of zone the opposition is employing. It can be a lot of fun and has a high success rate. Play is usually initiated within a few passes or one full rotation. Adding a name to 80 allows the players to be aware of what is to be run. The following figures are a few examples of the 80 format.

80 Drop

RESPONSIBILITIES

- **3**—Starts the play and draws D2 out to play him. Passes to 5 and reads the play.
- **5**—Plays at the 4 position, moves the ball to 1, and reads the play.
- **1**—On receiving the ball, looks to 6 on the high post first, and then passes the ball to 2.
- **2**—Plays between the crease line and the pipe. On receiving the ball, he must look up quickly to 6, who will be open momentarily. This is due to D1, who is returning from covering 1, and also D6, who has moved out of position to cover 4 on the diagonal cut.
- **4**—Plays a high crease, about five yards up and on the left side of the crease. As the ball is moved from 1 to 2, 4 drives diagonally to the offside crease, drawing D6 with him.
- **6**—As 5 passes to 1, 6 curls above 4 to a high-post position. He receives the ball from 1 if he is open. As the ball is passed to 2, 4 cuts on the diagonal. At this time, 6 drops straight down to the crease and expects a feed from 2.

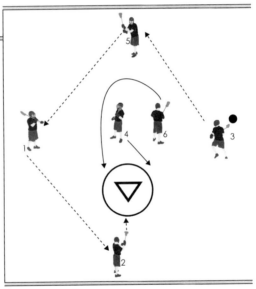

Figure 1.38 80 Drop

80 X

All the rules of 80 drop apply here, with the exception of the two crease players. Both play a high-crease position with the onside attackman moving first.

RESPONSIBILITIES

- **4**—As 2 is receiving the ball, he must cut hard, calling for the ball and drawing the crease defender, D6, to cover him.
- **6**—As 2 receives the ball, 6 must be alert of 4's cut to the goal. At that time, he quickly cuts off of 4's hip, driving to the opposite side. He remains open until D1 returns from covering 1.

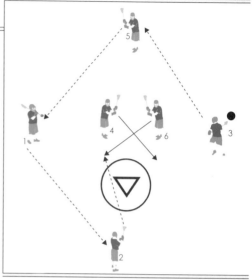

Figure 1.39 80 X

80 Scrape

This is a quick hitter from out of bounds, trying to catch the defense off guard. It can also be run out of the 2-2-2 formation with the attack in a full overload look.

RESPONSIBILITIES

- **2**—Brings the ball into play from out of bounds. 2 tries to draw a defender and then passes the ball to 1.
- **1**—Receives the ball from 2, and looks quickly to 6 running across the crease.
- **6**—As 1 receives the ball, 6 should be alert of the screen by 4 and run a scrape to the ball and down.
- **4**—On the pass to 1, 4 picks the next defender inside. That should be D6.
- **3**—Reads the play from an outside position. As 1 receives the ball, 3 cuts hard to the offside crease, anticipating a possible backdoor move.

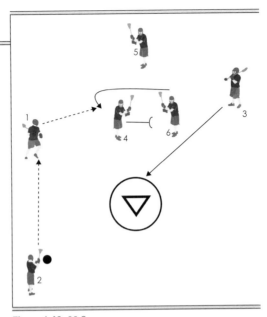

Figure 1.40 80 Scrape

80 Shorty

A technique in attacking the zone from the front is the 80 shorty move. It could be used as a progression move, with 4 taking the shot the first time it is run and 2 having that opportunity the next time around.

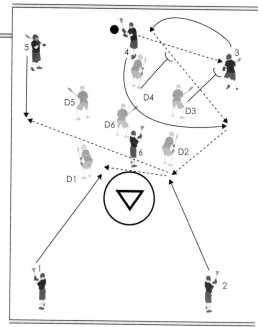

Figure 1.41 80 Shorty

RESPONSIBILITIES

- **4**—Begins the pattern in a three front at the 4 position. He draws attention from D4. 4 then passes the ball to 3, cuts down the middle halfway from the goal, and turns out toward the sideline, preparing to receive the ball from 3. D2 would be the defender responsible for 4. If D2 is caught sleeping and not doing his job, 4 should fire the shot. If D2 comes out to play him, 4 dumps the ball to 2 on the quick come-around.
- **3**—Receives the ball from 4 and fakes a sweep to his right. This should be just enough to draw D4, the backer, giving cushion to 4. 3 turns and passes back to 4, who should be in position to take the shot.
- **2**—As the play develops, 2 should sneak to the crease and prepare to receive the ball from 4 if 4 doesn't have the shot. 2, at this time, should take the shot or look to feed 1 or 5 on the offside crease.
- **1**—Stationed at the 1 position, 1 reads the progress of the play. He also comes to the offside crease, ready for the pass from 2.
- **5**—As the play develops, 5 slides down into a feeding lane, looking for a feed from 2.
- **6**—Applies a quick pop-out when 4 gets the ball, and should be alert of a possible pass from 2.

90 Series: Special Play Series

After scouting an opponent, it is sometimes important to employ an offense that may cause problems to the opposing team. This series is specifically set up for that purpose.

90 Buddy (Back Door)

In this scenario, the opposition has a strong tendency to defensively lean toward the ball. They are quite often unaware of the backdoor cut. The offense would want to take advantage of the situation by executing a backdoor look.

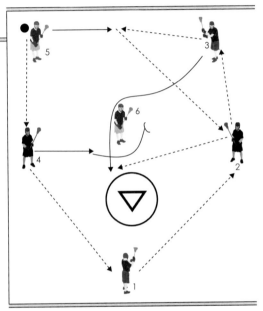

Figure 1.42 90 Buddy (Back Door)

RESPONSIBILITIES

- **5**—Starts ball movement to 4. After receiving the ball from 3, 5 carries to the 4 position and passes to 2.
- **3**—After passing to 5, 3 floats diagonally into an onside high post position. As 2 receives the ball, 3 backdoor cuts off of the double screen, looking for the feed and shot.
- **4**—Passes to 1 and floats to a diagonal double-crease position. He "loop screens" as 5 is passing to 2.
- **6**—Holds on a high (ten yards) crease. Must be aware and help on the buddy move.
- **2**—After receiving the ball from 5, 2 looks to feed 3 on the buddy cut.
- **1**—Moves the ball around from point position.

COACHING POINT *This play can be run comfortably from other formations.*

92 Easy

The 92 easy is an example of a play in the
90 series that can be beneficial to the team.
Though Figure 1.43 has the play starting at
the point position, it can also begin at the 5
or 3 position. This pattern is most effective
later in the contest as the opposing team
physically falters.

RESPONSIBILITIES

- **6**—Starts the pattern at the point position,
  possibly bringing the ball into play. He
  runs to the 2 plane position, turns to the
  outside, and passes the ball back to 1 at
  point behind. Once 1 runs a come-around
  to the 1 plane position, 6 assumes backup
  responsibilities at point behind.

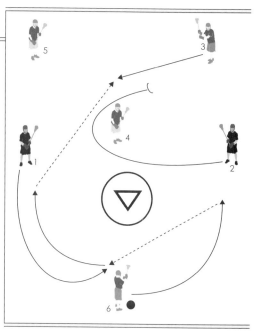

Figure 1.43 92 Easy

- **2**—As 6 approaches 2, 2 starts into the
  crease area, a stick length from 4 at a diagonal position.
  As 1 starts his come-around to the 1 plane, 2 circles around
  4 and sets up a screen halfway between 4 and 3.
- **1**—Starts at the 1 plane, fills for 6 at the vacated point position, receives the ball from 6, and begins his come-around
  to the 1 plane, looking to feed 3 on the cut.
- **3**—Begins at the 3 position and patiently waits for the
  come-around by 1. Cuts to the goal, scraping off of both
  2 and 4, looking for the feed.
- **4**—Plays on the crease, approximately five yards, trying to
  look important.
- **5**—Moves the ball along if it starts at his or 3's position.

Formations

24 Shorty

Quite often coaches feel very comfortable running certain formations that can cause havoc with the defense. A formation that has gained a great deal of attention with many teams is the 24 shorty formation. It is an attempt to constantly play the short-stick midfielders behind the cage. The reason is obvious. It is much easier to attack the goal from behind with the shorties. This is because of the possibilities of the individual one-on-one, or the force-and-dump. The 24 shorty can be run with two behind or with a spike man (the second man behind plays on the crease and backdoors as the iso man is coming around), as Figure 1.44 demonstrates.

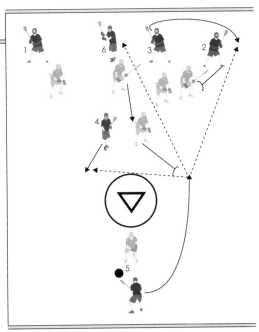

Figure 1.44 24 Shorty

RESPONSIBILITIES

- **5**—Secures the ball behind, penetrates to the strong side, looking to shoot or force and dump to 4, 3 on the Jack, or 6 up top.
- **4, spike man**—Plays center on the crease and backdoors when his man slides to support.
- **2**—Plays approximately twelve yards upfield and jacks when penetration is to his side.
- **3**—Plays five yards inside of 2 and curls outside for the shot when the Jack occurs.
- **6**—Must be prepared to get in the passing lane if his man supports the ball.
- **1**—Plays outside, approximately twelve yards, and supports the ball on the other side.

Shorty Diamond

A formation that seemed to always cause trouble for the opposition's defense is the shorty diamond. It's a simple formation to run and easy for players to learn. Because of its many combinations, the players always seem enthusiastic about it. The rules are very simple. Each player in the diamond is given a number. Their rules are:

- The *first number screens* and the *second number cuts* to the ball.
- If a player is not involved with the screen and cut, he makes an appropriate move.

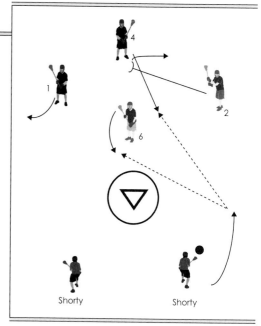

Figure 1.45 Shorty Diamond

42 Shorty

This is another formation style of play that patiently waits for the defense to run errant. Here the shorties are up top and have the option to power or dump off to the diagonal cut or the onside screen. It is important to note that the *offside outside man* is responsible for backing up on any onside shots.

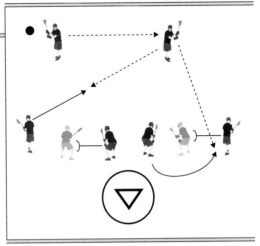

Figure 1.46 42 Shorty

The responsibilities can be many in this formation, depending on the offensive style of the coach. Other formations that are interesting to apply are the double-triple formation and the shooters formation. When used aggressively, these formation offenses can be very satisfying to the offensive coordinator. Simply by being creative, you can find quite a bit of offense when using this form of attack.

Three-Man Formation

One of the most respected and admired coaches in the game of lacrosse was coach Willis Bilderback, longtime head coach of the U.S. Naval Academy. For over a decade, through the '60s, coach Bildy dominated the game and had the intuition and nerve to change the traditional style of play with the inclusion of the isolation. Coach Bilderback would play his iso man behind the cage and line all the others in an I formation out front. It seemed that whatever the defense did in response, they were always wrong!

A few years later, the industrious Jerry Schmidt, highly successful head coach of Hobart College, developed a similar formation with a different approach. Coach Schmidt employed a three-man formation to one side of the crease, approximately stick-length apart, two behind the goal and a middie diagonally to the front of the three-man post. The attackman behind would force a come-around, either taking the shot or, in the case of an adjacent slide, dumping to the diagonal middie.

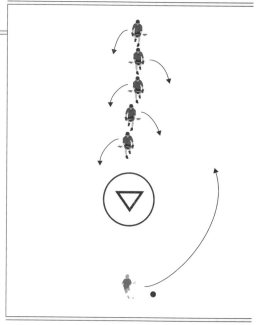

Figure 1.47 Three-Man Formation

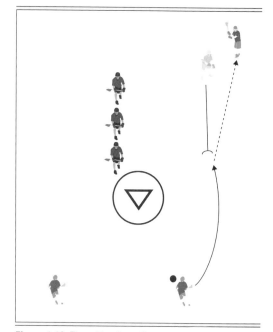

Figure 1.48 Three-Man Formation

Somewhat fascinated by the formation, especially the three-man technique and the havoc it played on the defenders, I felt a need to adopt it and increase the benefits. Thus the iso series became a favorite. Though it's on the borderline of "trash" lacrosse, I've always been amused at watching the defensive adjustments.

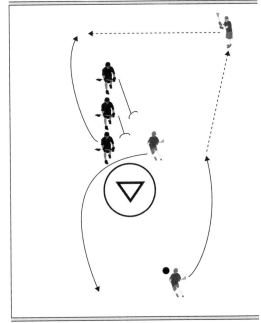

Figure 1.49 Three-Man Formation

Iso 3

For iso 3 to be effective, iso 1 or iso 2 must be run first. This automatically places the defenders between the ball and the three-man formation, allowing for the backdoor cut.

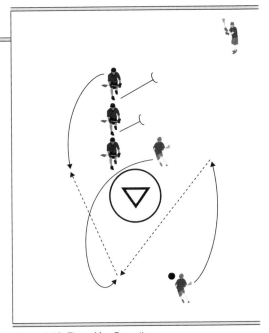

Figure 1.50 Three-Man Formation

Three-Man Formation

Having the courage to innovate, Tony Seaman, successful coach at Towson University, went a step further with the three-man pattern by aligning it across field instead of upfield. In his mode of play, the high-percentage shooters were placed on the outside of the group, two feeders or short-ies played behind on both sides, and the last player, a midfielder, was stationed up at the 4 position. The shooters were disciplined to take the high-percentage shots, with a quick release, to the far pipe, which would allow for a quick backup by the offside behind player. An unsuccessful attempt to one side would encourage a try from the other side.

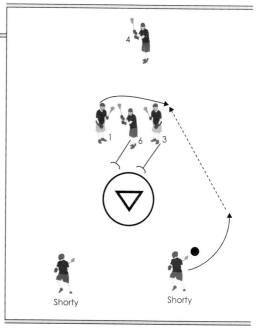

Figure 1.51 Three-Man Formation

Although the three-man offensive scheme may not be the style of play some coaches prefer, it should be appraised for the problems it causes defenders, at any level. Defenders become totally aware of the formation and question backup responsibilities. Should they support the ball or the three-man formation? Would it be best to play man-to-man or zone the formation? This slight pause, or hesitation, could be just what the doctor ordered for the offense. Offensive adjustments should be available and ready for use, depending on the defensive scheme employed (man-to-man or zone).

Shooters

The shooters offensive formation gives a great deal of concern to the defensive unit. There is the ability to (1) isolate from point behind or feed the double-screen–pop-out on the crease, (2) isolate from the wing or feed the double-screen–pop-out on the crease, or (3) isolate from the 4 position, feed the loop move on the crease, or both. To really be effective in this formation, it is important to try the come-around with the shooter or feeder first. This forces the defense covering the three-man to stay under and between the three-man formation and the goal. The defense becomes more concerned with the trick on the crease than they do with supporting the ball. When the ball is passed to the wing, the three defenders on the crease support the three-man formation more than the iso from the wing. If the defenders go to support the ball, the pop-out should be available. When the ball goes to the 4 position isolation, the three-man defenders are out of position to back the isolation up top. This allows the 4 position iso man an opportunity to beat only one defender. Shooters is a difficult formation to cover.

A team with a good feeder and a good iso man up top can gain great leverage with this formation.

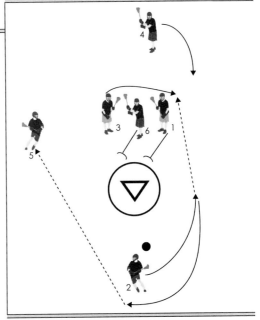

Figure 1.52 Shooters: Three-Man Iso or Feed

Extra-Man Offense

2

AT THE SAME CONTEST MENTIONED IN THE previous chapter, the North-South Classic at Cornell University, I made a game wager with Dick Edell. Back then, coaches and teachers did not have the pleasure of a paycheck coming in during the summer, and they had to find other part-time employment. My wife, Joan, and I opened a candy store in Ocean City, Maryland, that was located right on the boardwalk. We sold the best chocolates in town. And would you believe it, Dick Edell was one of our more frequent buyers. He really loved the cheaper candy. Just like today, he would never go deep into his pockets to buy the good stuff.

The night before the game, I told him if the South won, he would have to give me a pair of Army shorts and a T-shirt. I thought that he, being a Towson graduate, would opt for the Towson shorts and T-shirt, though I knew we didn't have a pair of shorts big enough for his big ass! I completely forgot about his outrageous appetite for sweet (cheap) candies. He retorted,

"I'll do it, but only for a box of your *best* chocolates." In my mind, there was no way we were going to lose—it seemed like a sure win. What I didn't take into consideration was the North's goalie, an athlete by the name of Rick Blick from Hobart College. This youngster thrived on pain—a pure masochist! If he didn't have fifteen or more welts on his body from shots after the game ended, he would go into a deep depression, whether the team won or lost. Legend has it that Blick derived pleasure by having lacrosse balls propelled at his rear end by a baseball pitching machine at a velocity of 75 miles an hour! (Obviously, that statement is not true; I just wanted to throw it in at this time.) We couldn't get even a laser beam by Blick. He stopped everything we threw at him and then would give us hell for not shooting harder. Near the end of the second quarter, with the score North 10, South 0, I called a time-out. As both teams huddled for instruction, I called Dick Edell to the middle of the field. "Rich, what kind of chocolates do you want?" He responded, "I'd like a box of the nonpareil truffles in dark chocolate." He picked the most expensive chocolate I had.

I told him I would throw in an extra pound of chocolates if he would bench Blick. He benched Blick! We were able to score a few in the second half, but we still lost the game. Later, I gave him a box of our best chocolates. I also went to the dollar store and picked up a box of cheap chocolates, placed them in one of our boxes, and gave them to the big turkey. He didn't know the difference between a good chocolate and an M and M!

The Extra-Man Offense

A phase of lacrosse that is unique and beautiful to watch is the extra-man offense (EMO) segment. One would believe that having an extra man involved in the offense would be a definite advantage, leaning toward a high scoring percentage, with the outcome being almost automatic. This is not the case, however, as defenses are designed to contest the situation with definite looks such as the five-man rotation, five-man zone, box-and-one, cutoffs, or any combination of such. Therefore, I am of the opinion that to increase the percentage of successful opportunities, a general understanding of the defenses is imperative to exploit any given situation. Many times coaches run a certain offensive set and have no idea as to what the defense is doing at the same time. How many times have players been asked to screen on certain plays and in trying to execute the given responsibility, missed or screened the wrong man? This has happened to all of us at one time or another and at all levels of play.

General EMO Principles

Place players in the proper position. As in basketball, it is imperative to have high-percentage players with the ball at the moment of finishing. Have your top players in the proper places at the proper times. Though you can culminate the play with the low-percentage shooter, it is in the best interest of the team to "go with your good stuff." Place feeders in the feeding positions, transporters in the transporting positions, and shooters where they can be most effective.

Use players who have good stickwork. For high-percentage play, it is best to use players with the best skills. Quite often the EMO is made up of some players who see the field only at this

53

time. In the long run, this is a good coaching move. It's not unusual to have a nonplayer possessing a cannon. If so, find a place for him.

Keep it simple. Some coaching involves going from one formation to another, with the ball being handled by many players many times. An example would be starting with a 3-3 offense, cutting to an open (sometimes called a zero or circle with no crease), then cutting to a 1-4-1, and when the ball gets behind at point, carrying to one side and filling the other side with a drop-off from the double crease, finally setting up in a 2-3-1. This isn't necessarily difficult, but it does involve a lot of ball transfer. Teams possessing the stickwork have no difficulty with this type of play. If a team is not blessed with this luxury, it should just set up in the 2-behind-3 across the crease—1 up top at the 4 position, or the 1-4-1 formation, and give the ball to Boomer!

Understand the defense. A simple example of this is observing how the defense plays a three front. Do they play the three offensive men up top with two defensive middies (a 3-2-type coverage) responsible for all three? Does the crease defenseman get involved when the ball is at the 4 position ("on a rope"), or does the defense play a diamond-style defense (1-3-1)? Being alert of these types of coverages can pay dividends quickly.

A sound philosophy in the EMO phase is to place the defensive unit in precarious positions that create difficulty in coverage. This can be accomplished in a number of ways. The formations can be transformed by player and ball movement—going from one formation to another and finally settling into the desired set. It may be the coach's feeling to just set up in the offensive pattern, which is difficult to handle, placing stress on the defense immediately. Time plays a key role in this phase of the game. It is important to be prepared to execute, whether you are limited to one minute, thirty seconds, or down to the last few ticks on the clock. The bottom line: be prepared!

At Towson we have always been of the opinion that offensive patterns should be dressed with certain elements that enhance the effectiveness of the situation. The following techniques and formations can be added to the EMO play and work to the advantage of the offense.

Screen Jack

This is highly effective in the EMO play, but is not used as much as it should be. The screen or pick can be very irritating to the defensive unit, whether executed on an all-even situation or a man-down play. A defender could be doing everything correctly in the coverage and still get caught unexpectedly by the technique. By applying a *code word* to the end of any given play, the screen can be put into action. In our terminology, *Jack* was the identifying word.

This technique positions a defender in a completely different area from where he usually plays. It forces the adjacent defenseman to make a quick adjustment once he realizes what has taken place.

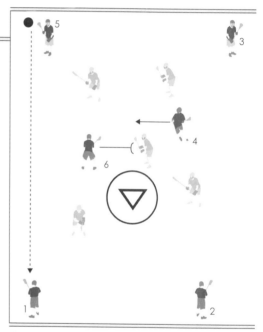

Figure 2.1 Screen Jack

Carry

RESPONSIBILITIES

- **1**—Playing point behind, passes to 2.
- **2**—Once covered by D2, carries the ball up to the 3 position.
- **6**—Fills quickly at the vacated 2 position, and waits for a return pass from 2. Once he receives the ball, he looks to either shoot or dump the ball to 1 on the sneak.
- **4**—Curls to a high-post position above where 6 was.
- **5**—Comes into a backdoor position, while 3 finds a comfort zone between his position and 5. 1, with the ball, can also feed 5 or 3.

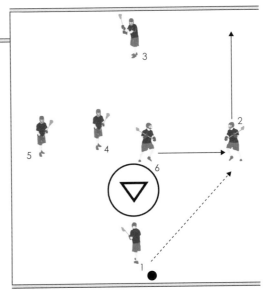

Figure 2.2 Carry

This is just one example of moving the defensemen around to different positions. The carry can also be used at point behind or the 4 position up top. It is an excellent technique to gain or keep the advantage.

Follow

The follow technique is used when defenders react quickly by anticipating the next pass. In this situation:

- 4 throws the ball to 1.
- 1 fakes a throw to the next player in the rotation and returns the ball to player 4, who is cutting to the goal.

The follow technique can be used successfully at the corners, at topside, and at the point, as in the 1-4-1 formation.

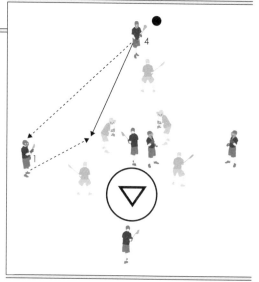

Figure 2.3 Follow

2-3-1

The 2-3-1 (two behind, three wide across the crease, one at the 4 position) and the offensive sets to follow all place stress on man-down units.

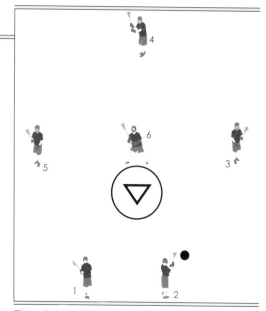

Figure 2.4 2-3-1

2-4 Regular

This EMO offensive setup is an excellent formation that places undue stress on the defensive unit. Anytime the unit places two men behind, as in the 2-4 formation, the defense is responsible to cover each man individually. This in turn forces the remaining three defenders to cover four offensive players stretched across the front. The offense can now jack either the outside man or the inside man. There are numerous alternatives in this formation.

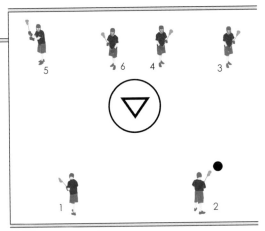

Figure 2.5 2-4 Regular

2-4 Stack

Again, with two offensive players behind and a diagonal stack in front of the crease, the EMO unit has the same tricks available as in the 2-4 regular. Important here is the timing between the stacked players and the attack position.

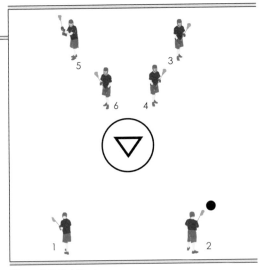

Figure 2.6 2-4 Stack

Overload (Short Time)

This is an excellent formation to be used with just a little time remaining on the clock. When executed properly, the offense forces coverage on the onside players, leaving but one defender to cover the offside.

Figure 2.7 Overload (Short Time)

Double-Triple

The double-triple is technically a difficult formation to cover. It has many options available and gives the offensive crew the ability to freelance if nothing else.

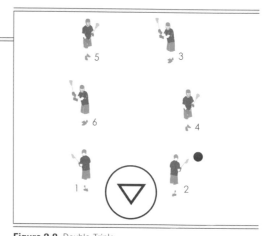

Figure 2.8 Double-Triple

4-2 (Load)

With a two-front formation, the 4-2 set forces a two-man defensive coverage and enables the lower four players to apply the Jack technique from the onside two or the offside two. It can easily be converted to a double-triple and then to a 2-4 regular. The bottom line: it plays havoc on the defense!

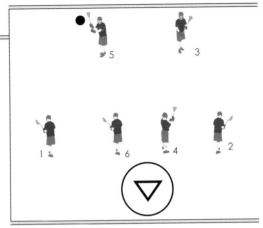

Figure 2.9 4-2 (Load)

Adjusting to the Defensive Coverage

As previously stated, for the proper offensive set to be effective, it is very important that the offense recognize the employed defensive mode. The following are just a few simple adjustments found to be effective against certain coverages.

Man-Down Defense, Box-and-One, or Two-Front Zone vs. 3-3 Regular (EMO)

Force D5 to play the ball at the 5 position, which in turn forces D3 to play 4. Change the formation slightly from a 3-3 regular to a 3-3 tight, as shown in Figure 2.10, by dropping the wings down about seven yards and bringing the attack to the crease wings. This eventually forces the close defense to rotate out.

RESPONSIBILITIES
- **3** and **5**—Are shooters.
- **4**—Is a feeder to 1 and 2.
- **1, 2, or both**—Feed 6.

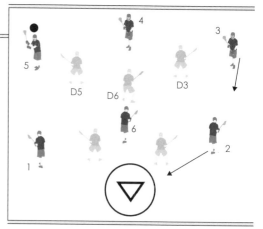

Figure 2.10 Man-Down Defense, Box-and-One, or Two-Front Zone vs. 3-3 Regular (EMO)

33 Tight (Adjustment)

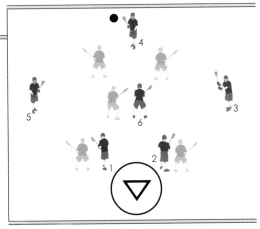

Figure 2.11 33 Tight (Adjustment)

Man-Down Defense, Box-and-One, or Two-Front vs. 1-3-2

It is important to recognize the close defenders with double responsibilities. Example: With D1 responsible for both 1 and 6, and D2 having the same responsibilities on the other side, it would be advantageous to work the ball up top at the 3 and 5 positions, with 5 passing to 1. At this time, D1 would pick up 1, and as 1 passes the ball to 6 at point behind, D1 releases and returns to his E position, playing 6 in a soft technique. 6 should now be alert to return the ball to 1 for the shot (follow technique).

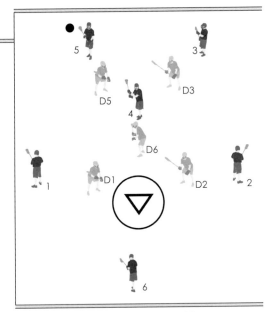

Figure 2.12 Man-Down Defense, Box-and-One, or Two-Front vs. 1-3-2

3

Defense

SOME OF THE MOST DIFFICULT TIMES IN MY
coaching career occurred while I was coaching the University of
Arizona lacrosse teams during the '60s. The players were great
to work with and a fantastic bunch of young men. The difficulty involved
traveling to play contests. The closest game was Arizona State up at
Tempe, which was 135 miles away. The next closest contest was at
Los Angeles, California, which was about 450 miles away. After
that, mileage was based on hours. Twenty-two hours to the
Air Force Academy, and approximately eighteen-plus hours
to Salt Lake City, Utah. The contests were always games
with multiple teams. For example, we would leave
Tucson early Thursday morning, play the Air Force
Academy on Friday, play University of Colorado
on Saturday, and play Denver University
at 9:00 A.M. Sunday morning. Then we
would leave right after the game, hopefully before noon, and head home.

The camaraderie was overwhelming. Because of the allocated low

budgets, home teams were responsible for the housing and feeding of the visiting players. Without this kind of support, it would have been impossible to have a full season of play. Funds for our travel meals were provided by donations from local lacrosse enthusiasts. With a caravan of four vehicles—station wagons—we would drive half a day, stop in a small town, and eat. I would go into a supermarket, buy the meat, cheese, condiments, several loaves of bread, and soft drinks. The food was laid out on one of the station wagons with the meat, cheese, condiments, and bread placed on the hood of the car, and the soft drinks placed on the laid-down rear door. The order was easy: told to "circle the wagons," the players were to circle the car until all the food was gone, at which time we loaded back up to finish the trip.

On a return trip from Boulder, Colorado, with the drivers very sleepy, I signaled to stop at the next rest stop or town to take a nap for fifteen to twenty minutes. We were coming into a small town in New Mexico named Truth or Consequences, at about 3:00 A.M. Since there were no streetlights, everything was totally dark. I saw a large parking lot, which I assumed was a supermarket, and beckoned the other cars to park and take that nap. I'm not sure how long we slept, but I remember being awakened by bright lights in my face and being prodded with a stick. The driver of each car was being questioned by the state police as to what our intentions were. I tried to explain we represented the University of Arizona and that we were on our way back to Tucson when we decided to stop and take a nap. The police officers were confused and wanted to know what the hell we were going to use the sticks for. After trying to explain the sport of lacrosse, it was unanimously decided that we should move on and stop at the rest stop a few miles outside of town. As we left the lot, I saw the large sign in front of the building. We hadn't stopped at a shopping mart—rather, we had parked in the lot of the local bank. The officers actually thought we were going to rob the bank!

Regular Defense: Man-to-Man

Jerry Schmidt, longtime successful coach in the game of lacrosse, was a coach to be respected. His innovations in game structure totally changed the game. In the early '70s, Jerry's teams would harass the opponent unmercifully with the aggressive man-to-man double-team package that is so popular today. His teams were also the first to employ all long-sticks in defending against clears, along with being the first to use an exclusive defensive midfield unit on the defensive end of the field.

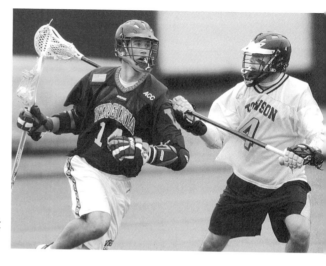

Many coaches at all levels in the game of lacrosse today enjoy and employ Jerry's innovations.

Without a doubt, defense is the single most important phase of the game of lacrosse. Good defense is only about 20 percent technique. The other 80 percent is measured by a desire to succeed, which comes from great determination and intensity. Along with determination, other important components involve aggressiveness (a team playing with winning as its ultimate goal), and pride, which is the culmination of determination, aggressiveness, and conditioning. Players must be able to hustle, scrap, and *physically extend* themselves, with an above-average effort.

Man-to-man defense can easily give players the impression that their responsibility is to cover only the player whom they are assigned: "I'll help you if I can, but I have to watch my man!" Nothing could be further from the truth. There is no such thing as man-to-man defense. Technically, the man covering the ball is man-to-man, with the other players reading any type of offensive threat and being in a position to react accordingly. Many coaches teach this phase of the game by breaking down the responsibilities of players and how these responsibilities can change at any time. Though coaches may have their own names for different positions and techniques, the following terms are appropriate:

- **Cover.** This is the man playing the ball, also referred to as the "force." If the ball is at the corners, the 3 or 5 positions, the cover man will station himself to the inside of the ball, disallowing any sweeps and forcing the ball down the side. If the ball is at the 4 position, the cover will take away the strong stick side and force the ball to the weak stick side.
- **Hot.** This is the player responsible for creating the double-team backup. He is usually the next man closest to the ball, sometimes referred to as the "near" man. At the start of offensive penetration, he releases to support the cover man. His angle of pursuit should be to the point of attack. He should lead with his stick first and body next, being alert to return to his normal position at the appropriate time or assume the role of the cover.
- **Backer.** Probably the most important defensive player is the player who supports the hot man. In this game, offensive players react to where the initial slide comes from. Backers have been drilled from early on to force and dump when they play. All defensive players must distinguish where they fit in on the slide to the ball. Players must talk with the adjacent defensive players. Without communication, any defense will totally lose its effectiveness. It is a must!
- **Fill.** This player is usually the offside defensive midfielder. He is the third man of the defensive triangle. He will crash to the offside hole area, looking for the first open man generally vacated by the backer. Since his job is so difficult, it is important to run reaction drills daily to improve the situation.

- **Match up.** This is the call given to the player covering the ball. It informs him that a defender is in pursuit. Most likely, this defender is the hot man. On the "match up" call, the cover releases, turns quickly, and picks up the first open player, usually on the crease. He returns to his normal coverage at the appropriate time.
- **Bite 'em.** When the hot defender is in pursuit of the ball and feels the double can be effective, he gives the "bite 'em" call. Both players work hard to take the ball away and *not* let the offensive player feed or pass.
- **Choke.** Sometimes it is more advantageous for the wing defenseman to cross over the front of the goal and "match up" or "bite 'em." The close wing defenders use this move. At times, it is more appropriate than a slide from the crease or adjacent middie.
- **Angle.** This term is used to inform the defender covering the ball to play or shade to the strength side of the offensive player. This gives the defender the opportunity to decide the direction taken by the offensive player.
- **Lock on.** Also referred to as "cut off" or "hold," the lock-on usually occurs adjacent to the double team, forcing the ball carrier to make the more difficult pass or feed.
- **Prerotate.** Quite often defensive players are asked to prerotate, or slide away from the man they are covering, being alert to slide to the next open player.

Man-to-Man vs. 2-2-2 Iso at the 3 Position

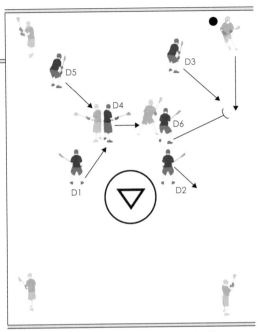

Figure 3.1 Man-to-Man vs. 2-2-2 Iso at the 3 Position

RESPONSIBILITIES

- **D3**—Positioned at an inside shade to discourage any sweep move. Forces the ball down the side, and does not give up the inside position. Must listen for the "match up" or "bite 'em" call and respond accordingly.
- **D6**—He is the near man and is ready to read and release. He takes a proper angle of pursuit, driving his stick through the front of the offensive player. He is responsible for determining the "match up" or "bite 'em" call.
- **D4**—As the backer, he must be ready to slide to the vacated player. This is an important read and must be executed. A breakdown here could be very costly.
- **D5**—Being adjacent to the ball, he will sluff in, be aware of his man while also watching the ball, and prepare to fill quickly to the offside crease. He is the third man in the defensive backside triangle.
- **D2**—Supports at the A position. Can also apply the "cut off" call at the 2 position.
- **D1**—Supports at the E position. Could be called on to support the area vacated by D4.

Man-to-Man vs. 2-2-2 Iso at the 2 Position

RESPONSIBILITIES

- **D2**—Takes a shade position, and forces the ball upfield. Must be alert for calls made by the hot man.
- **D6**—As hot man, he watches his man and also the ball. He is quick to release to force the ball. Must alert D2 about what to do.
- **D4**—On the release of D6, he immediately slides to the next man.
- **D3**—Sluffs in and can also cut off.
- **D5**—Reads the slide and fills down to the open man.
- **D1**—Supports at the E position, and helps on offside crease.

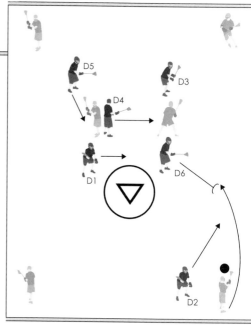

Figure 3.2 Man-to-Man vs. 2-2-2 Iso at the 2 Position

Man-to-Man vs. 2-2-2 Iso at Point

RESPONSIBILITIES

- **D4**—Is responsible for the ball and forces toward the weak stick side. Must be alert to any calls given by the hot or near man.
- **D6**—In this situation, he is the near man and should call out that he is hot. Should give the "fire" sound when he releases to force the ball.
- **D2**—Goes to a hold mode. If ball comes out farther, he would be the near man.
- **D1**—Needs to be ready to react to D6's move and slide across to replace him. May also be needed as the choke man.
- **D3**—Supports the crease if needed, and is ready for the diagonal pass.
- **D5**—Sluffs off and reacts to support the offside crease on the "fire" call.

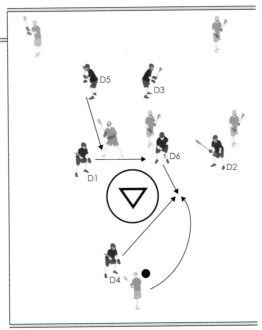

Figure 3.3 Man-to-Man vs. 2-2-2 Iso at Point

Man-to-Man vs. 1-3-2 Iso at 2 Plane (Wing)

RESPONSIBILITIES

- **D2**—Plays an angle position to the strong side of the ball carrier.
- **D6**—Is quick to release to the ball if the ball carrier goes to the back line side. If the ball should go upfield, D3 would be the hot man and D6 would support crease area.
- **D4**—Holds or cuts off at point.
- **D3**—If the ball goes under, he maintains support at the C position. If the ball comes toward him, he becomes the hot man.
- **D5**—Sluffs in and remembers he must fill if D1 should release to the crease.
- **D1**—Supports offside at E position. Stays alert to slide by D6 and reacts.

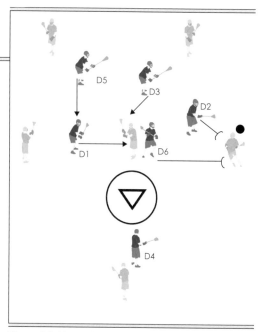

Figure 3.4 Man-to-Man vs. 1-3-2 Iso at 2 Plane (Wing)

Alternate Slide with Ball Coming Under at 2 Plane (Wing)

RESPONSIBILITIES

- **D2**—Responsible for the ball. Pressures and does not allow ball upfield.
- **D4**—Becomes the near man and attacks the ball. Player must remember that communication is important here.
- **D6**—Supports at the crease position.
- **D1**—Must read the situation, supporting the offside crease unless he feels the next pass might go to the point.
- **D5**—Supports at the D position and is on call; slides to fill for D1.
- **D3**—Supports at the B position. Must be ready to attack the diagonal pass.

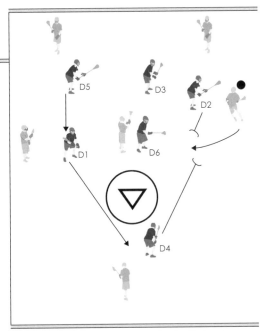

Figure 3.5 Alternate Slide with Ball Coming Under at 2 Plane (Wing)

Man-to-Man vs. 1-3-2 Iso at Point—Angle

RESPONSIBILITIES

- **D4**—First responsibility is to play the proper angle. Forces the ball and listens for call by near man.
- **D6**—On penetration by ball, takes proper angle of pursuit, reads situation, and makes call for D4.
- **D1**—On ball movement, D1 prepares to back for D6.
- **D5**—Supports the D area and must be ready to fill for D1.
- **D2**—Supports by cutting off at his position.
- **D3**—Maintains position at the B area.

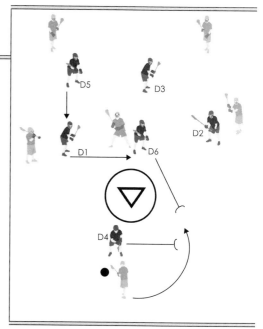

Figure 3.6 Man-to-Man vs. 1-3-2 Iso at Point—Angle

Man-to-Man vs. 1-3-2 Iso at Point—Choke

RESPONSIBILITIES

- **D4**—Takes away the strong side, and applies a heavy force in coverage.
- **D1**—Is ready to react to a predetermined call ("choke 'em").
- **D5**—After hearing the "choke 'em" call, D5 automatically knows he is responsible for quickly filling the vacated spot left by D1.
- **D6**—Is responsible for the crease.
- **D2**—Holds at the 2 plane.
- **D3**—Maintains a position at the B area, and should be alert for the diagonal pass.

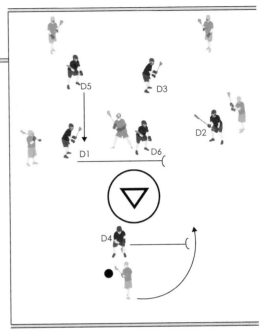

Figure 3.7 Man-to-Man vs. 1-3-2 Iso at Point—Choke

Man-to-Man vs. 1-4-1 Iso at Point

Though there are a few ways to defend the iso at point, the most practical, from the previous play (Figure 3.7), is to apply the choke technique. There would be only one backer, D5. All others lock on.

RESPONSIBILITIES

- **D4**—First priority is to play the angles and take away the strong stick side, and D4 forces the ball to the weak side, applying heavy pressure. Listens for the hot man and reacts accordingly.
- **D1**—Is prepared to choke. Does not allow the iso man to get to the goal or to feed.
- **D5**—Slides quickly to the offside crease to cover the man vacated by D1.
- **D6**—Maintains a hold position at the onside crease.
- **D2**—Supports the onside wing area. D2 cannot allow his man to receive the ball if iso man is forced to pass.
- **D3**—Supports at the C position.

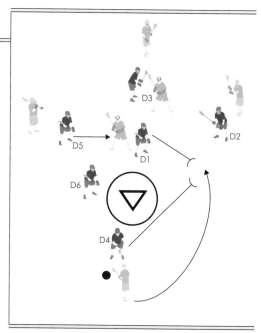

Figure 3.8 Man-to-Man vs. 1-4-1 Iso at Point

Man-to-Man vs. 1-4-1 Iso at 4

RESPONSIBILITIES

- **D4**—With the ball at the 4 position, D4 plays the strong angle on the ball.
- **D6**—Becomes the hot man, and pressures the ball, trying to take him out of his offensive mode.
- **D1**—Holds on the offside crease, and watches for any pass to sneak from behind.
- **D2**—Has a very important function. If he is responsible for the point man, he plays on the opposite side of the D4 (playing the angle). This allows an immediate slide to be available.
- **D3**—Holds at the 2 plane position, and must be aware of a feed to the point man sneaking on his side.
- **D5**—Plays an offside hold. Must also be aware of a feed to the point man sneaking around his side.

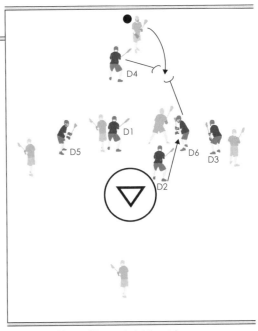

Figure 3.9 Man-to-Man vs. 1-4-1 Iso at 4

Isolation Defense: Iso-Black Front

As a matter of defensive philosophy, I have always had the opinion that anytime an opposing team goes into an "isolation at the 4 position or point behind," the iso defender should be supported by an automatic zone formation. The players would line up in a 1-2-3 formation with the long-stick playing behind the iso defender to the strength side of the offensive player, since this is the player wanted as the first backer. As soon as the isolation is detected, all players call out, "Iso black!" Once this situation has changed, the players regroup immediately to their previous coverage.

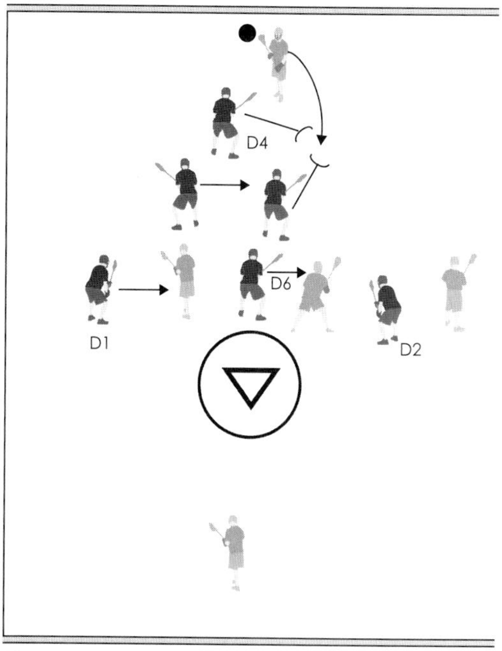

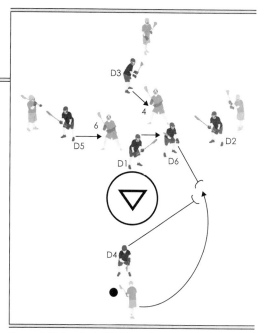

Figure 3.10 Iso-Black Front

Iso Black at Point

As previously stated, once the offensive formation is detected, a call of "iso black" is given and the defending players move quickly to the iso-black zone formation. The slide should come early with the closest inside defender releasing to the ball. D4, the iso defender, must work to cover the ball with no cushion, remembering the importance of not letting the iso attack-middie pass the ball to the offside wing player.

Figure 3.11 Iso Black at Point

77

Zone Defense

4

HOW MANY TIMES IN COACHING HAS THE WRONG message been sent at the most inappropriate time? We've all experienced this in one way or another. With the team up by a goal or two, and little time on the clock, the coach calls a time-out to make sure every player understands the situation. After a thorough explanation, the players take the field and execute something that has never been seen before! Most embarrassing is trying to convince the spectators later on that what the youngsters ran in the game was not what was discussed in the time-out. The following are examples of this scenario.

In a hard-fought game against the U.S. Naval Academy a few years ago, with a minute left and the score tied, I called a time-out to organize our defense. We knew Navy would go with their best offensive threat, and we decided to force them out of their offense somewhat by running a zone. I explicitly went over the zone we would run and felt confident it would confuse the offense. As we broke the huddle, the players ran to the field to take their positions. Unfortunately, one of our defenders, somewhat of an airhead, was shouting very loudly, "I've got number 24!" I knew then we were in a lot of trouble. It was a very long bus ride back home!

Another time, during the NCAA semifinals a few years back, Towson had a great bunch of talented youngsters and was playing Maryland. If we won the contest, we would play in the finals. It was a very exciting time. The clock showed approximately three minutes remaining with Towson leading by three goals. We were bringing the ball inbounds on the offensive end, from inside the restraining line, in a dead-ball situation. Trying to look like I knew what the heck I was doing, I called a time-out. In the huddle, I explained to the players that we wanted to hold onto the ball, so we could force Maryland to come after us with either a single defender or the double and possibly get fouled in the process. This would give us the one-minute EMO cushion, and if we didn't screw things up, we would be going to the finals.

The player bringing the ball inbounds was a very competent lacrosse player, but unfortunately he was mentally similar to the earlier defender who had number 24. At the sound of the whistle, he drove straight to the goal and shot the ball . . . directly and perfectly into the goalie's stick. I have never been as upset with a player as I was at that time. I did, however, benefit from this ordeal to a great extent, through monthly visits to my cardiologist.

The Zone Defense

The zone defense has been an important part of our defensive philosophy. Many coaches have held the belief that you teach one defense and perfect it. If the recruiting year has been successful, this may be the way to go. It was my belief that implementing the zone defense would benefit my team's defensive structure. I was originally influenced by Howdy Myers of Hofstra University through watching his team play well against outstanding teams while employing the zone defense. The consistency of the box scores always being low, along with the pressure placed on the offense and individual players throughout the game, was meaningful. It was definitely the way to go. The next move was to decide which defensive structure to accept. The Howdy Myers zone was incorporated from the early basketball five-man zone philosophy. It was an efficient defensive weapon, but since Hofstra was on our schedule, why should we adopt a zone they would be very familiar with and have practiced against all season? Thus our acceptance of the Towson, or the double backer, zone.

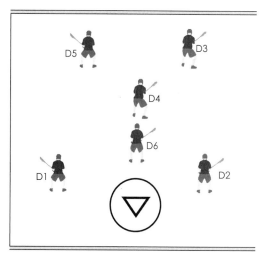

Figure 4.1 The Zone Defense

General Zone Defense Rules

The players need to be aware of the following zone defense rules:

- **See the man in your area.** Players should always be alert to the positioning of the player(s) in their area. It is essential that possible advantage moves by the offense are discouraged and eliminated. This would include backdoor cuts,

81

passes, or picks. The defenseman must always be aware of his opponent's positioning.

- **Know where the ball is.** The defenseman's responsibilities are determined by the position and movement of the ball. Therefore, it is important for him to watch ball movement and adjust accordingly.
- **Know your responsibilities.** There are definite requirements for each defenseman within the zone package. For the total defensive scheme to be successful, each defenseman must have an understanding of the zone defense being run, along with his own responsibilities.
- **Anticipate backing and sliding.** Each defenseman must recognize the situation and react immediately. He should mentally anticipate the possibilities of the offense—his reaction time depends upon it.
- **Communicate.** The most important phase of any defensive set is communication; it is the catalyst of a successful defense. Players should always encourage and inform their teammates. Communication is the extra man of defense.

Teaching the Zone

To properly teach the six-man zone defense, familiarize the players with both the four-man and five-man schemes first. This avoids duplication. Many coaches find no problem in teaching the four-, five-, and six-man techniques with different rotations. Basically, this is the coach's preference. My intention has always been to keep the defensive rotation, within the three schemes, as relative as possible, eliminating double learning and saving precious practice time.

Sometimes, however, certain adjustments must be recognized to implement a stronger game plan. To establish a sound defensive structure, it is important to initiate the defense from a very basic look. In teaching the zone, I have found the best approach to this defense philosophy is the use of progression. The zone is started with the four-man rotation. After the confidence level has improved somewhat, it is advanced with the five-man rotation and finally the six-man game. The following are examples of the progressive teaching scheme.

Four-Man Rotation

Two popular formations are the box and diamond setups. Both are dictated by the offensive formation. A good rule to follow is that if the opposition shows a two front, players at the 3 and 5 positions, then the best four-man would be the box (see Figure 4.2), whereas the diamond would be better suited to a three or one front (see Figure 4.3).

Four vs. Two Front (Box)

RESPONSIBILITIES
- **D4**—Picks up the ball.
- **D6**—Plays at the C position, anticipates a pass to 5, and is alert to inside movement.
- **D1**—Plays the E position, and communicates with D6 about inside movement.
- **D2**—Plays the A position, anticipates a pass to 2, and supports the crease.

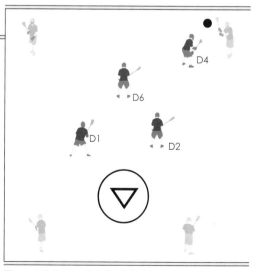

Figure 4.2 Four vs. Two Front (Box)

Four vs. One Front (Diamond Coverage)

The ball starts at the 3 position.

RESPONSIBILITIES
- **D4**—Picks up the ball.
- **D6**—Plays the X position, supporting the ball and the high crease.
- **D2**—Plays the A position, supporting D4 and the crease.
- **D1**—Plays the E position, supporting D4 and the crease.

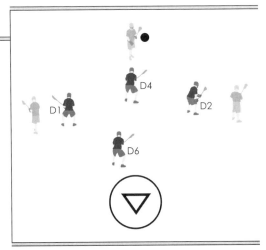

Figure 4.3 Four vs. One Front (Diamond Coverage)

3 Passes to 5

RESPONSIBILITIES
- **D6**—Picks up the ball.
- **D4**—Drops in quickly to the B position, facing the ball and supporting the high crease.
- **D1**—Plays the E position, anticipates a pass to 1, and supports the crease.
- **D2**—Plays the A position, supports the crease, and communicates with D4.

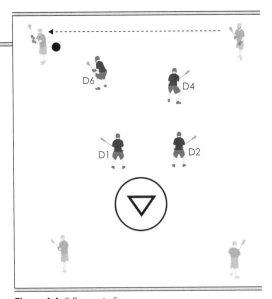

Figure 4.4 3 Passes to 5

5 Passes to 1

RESPONSIBILITIES

- **D1**—Plays a "soft" technique (no pressure). D1 does not release until D6 returns.
- **D6**—Quickly returns to the E+ position, giving support to the inside.
- **D2**—Supports the crease from the X position.
- **D4**—Supports the A+ area, and must be available to support at the E+ if needed. On the pass from 5 to 1, if D6 is slow to get back or the D+ area is open, D4 and D6 could also switch positions if needed.

All players are responsible for any diagonal passes.

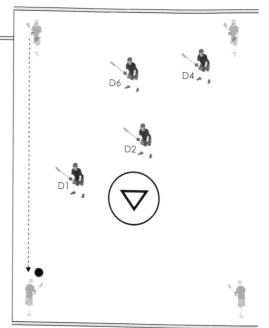

Figure 4.5 5 Passes to 1

1 Passes to 2

RESPONSIBILITIES

- **D2**—Hesitates in picking up the ball, and plays a soft technique.
- **D1**—Comes back to the X in a support mode.
- **D4**—Faces the ball at the A+ position, and supports inside.
- **D6**—Supports the E+ area, and must be available to support at the A+ if needed.

All players are responsible for any diagonal passes.

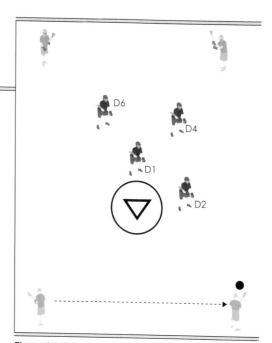

Figure 4.6 1 Passes to 2

2 Passes to 3

Everyone returns to the original formation.

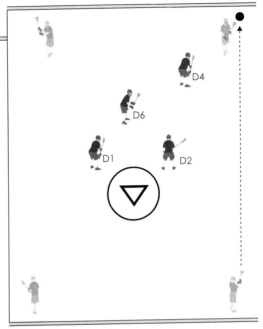

Figure 4.7 2 passes to 3

Diamond Coverage

Diamond Alignment (1-4-1) vs. 2-1-3

BASIC ALIGNMENT AND RESPONSIBILITIES

- **D4**—Picks up the ball at the 4 area.
- **D1**—Plays at the E+ position, and anticipates a pass to the 5 position.
- **D2**—Plays at the A+ position, and anticipates a pass to the 3 position.
- **D6**—Plays at the X position, and supports
  the crease.

All players are responsible for any diagonal
passes.

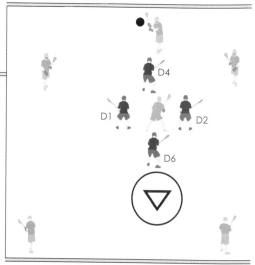

Figure 4.8 Diamond Alignment vs. 2-1-3

4 Passes to 5

RESPONSIBILITIES

- **D1**—Picks up the ball at the 5 position.
- **D4**—Gets back to the D position to support D1 and the high crease.
- **D6**—Slides to the E position, supporting D2 and anticipating an onside pass to 1.
- **D2**—Slides to the A+ position, supporting the crease and helping until D4 returns.

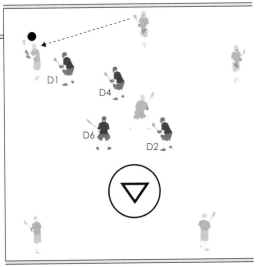

Figure 4.9 4 Passes to 5

5 Passes to 1

RESPONSIBILITIES

- **D6**—Picks up the ball, and plays a soft technique.
- **D1**—Slides back to the D position, and supports the inside game.
- **D2**—Slides to the E position, supports D6, and has crease responsibilities.
- **D4**—Slides to the A position when released by D1.

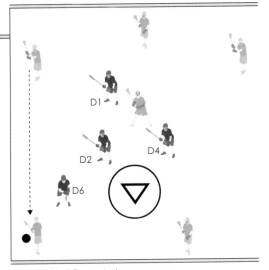

Figure 4.10 5 Passes to 1

1 Passes to 2

RESPONSIBILITIES

- **D2**—Picks up the ball, and plays a soft technique.
- **D6**—Returns to the X position on the crease.
- **D4**—Slides to the B+ position, supporting the crease and anticipating the next pass.
- **D1**—Slides to the C position, supporting the high crease; diagonals and communicates.

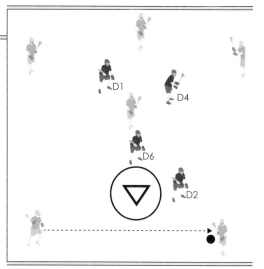

Figure 4.11 1 Passes to 2

2 Passes to 3

RESPONSIBILITIES

- **D4**—Picks up the ball.
- **D2**—Slides back to the A position, supports the crease, and backs D4.
- **D1**—Plays the C position, supports the high crease, and anticipates the next pass.
- **D6**—Slides to the E+ position, and has crease responsibilities.

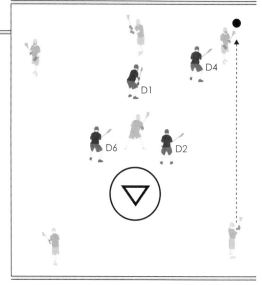

Figure 4.12 2 Passes to 3

3 Passes to 4

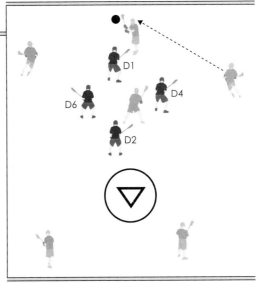

Figure 4.13 3 Passes to 4

RESPONSIBILITIES
- **D1**—Has the ball at the 4 position.
- **D4**—Slides back to the B+ position, supporting D1 and the crease.
- **D2**—Slides to X when released by D4, and has crease responsibilities.
- **D6**—Holds at the E+ position, supporting the ball and the crease.

At this time, the four-man defensive unit has made a complete rotation. Anytime an offensive player is positioned in the 4 area, this is referred to as a "one" front. The best coverage for that type of offense is the diamond formation, where the defensemen are positioned in a diamond shape. Once the ball is in movement, the defensive rotation within either set is the same. Quite often, teams disregard this principle and find themselves placed in a vulnerable position. It's bad enough to be two men down without also increasing the opportunity for scoring by contributing to the offensive cause.

COACHING POINT   *In the four-man zone, the defense should always be in a 1-2-1 formation facing the ball, regardless of formation.*

Five-Man Rotation

Though there are many schemes for playing the five-man game, at Towson we have found a comfort zone playing two ways:

- Box-and-one
- Full five-man zone

We have used both successfully in contests as a matter of change-ups, trying to give the offensive team something else to think about, while hoping to disturb the offensive continuity. Basically, these defenses would be implemented during the man-down situations.

Box-and-One

In this defensive set, the four-man zone can be applied and the fifth man can be placed at different areas to harass the offensive continuity. If a coach has inexperienced players, he may place the fifth man, or weakest defender, on the crease with only crease responsibilities, using the strongest four defensemen for the rotation.

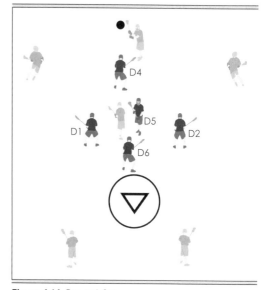

Figure 4.14 Box-and-One

The fifth man can also be used as a cutoff man, playing a tight man-to-man position on a selected offensive player or position. The remaining four defenders continue their game following the rules set up in the four-man zone, regardless of the offensive formation. Food for thought: never play your best defender as the fifth man.

This is another look at the box-and-one. In this scenario, the rover plays the attackman behind the cage at the point position. The basic four defenders apply the same rules for coverage that were applied in the four-man coverage package.

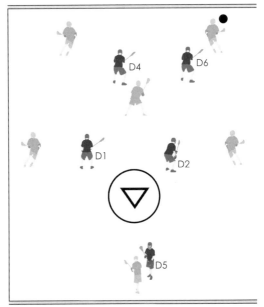

Figure 4.15 Box-and-One: Rover at Point Position

Full Five-Man Zone

The five-man zone is the basic defense used in the man-down situation. It is a very cerebral defense, calling for each defender to rise to a new level of play. The key element for this defense to be successful is called the one-man-behind principle. When this principle is observed, D6 is always responsible for the man at point behind, while D1 and D2 hold their respective positions supporting the ball.

This coverage can also take the presence of a 1-3-1. The adjacent-man rotation would be enforced here.

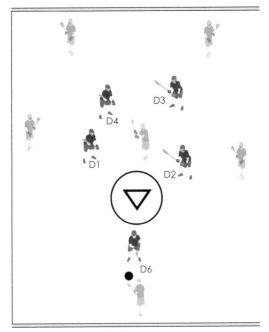

Figure 4.16 Full Five-Man Zone

Another rule for success is that D3 and D4 form a "triangular" relationship with D6.

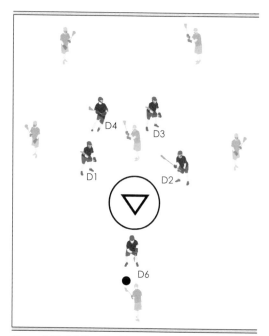

Figure 4.17 Full Five-Man Zone: D3-D4-D6 Triangle

The prerotated 1-3-1 provides an alternate coverage look within the full five-man zone.

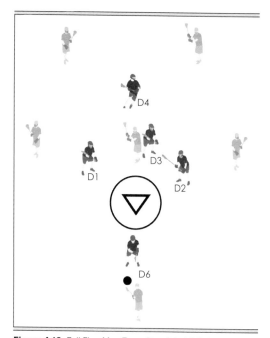

Figure 4.18 Full Five-Man Zone: Prerotated 1-3-1

Five-Man Zone vs. 1-3-2

The ball starts at the 3 position.

RESPONSIBILITIES

- **D3**—Picks up the ball at the 3 position.
- **D6**—Supports D3 at the B position.
- **D4**—Supports the high crease and D6 at the D position.
- **D1**—Supports the low crease at the E+ position, and watches 1 and D4.
- **D2**—Supports the A position.

All are responsible for diagonal pass.

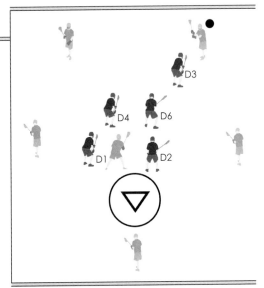

Figure 4.19 Five-Man Zone vs. 1-3-2

3 Passes to 5

RESPONSIBILITIES

- **D4**—Picks up the ball at 5 position.
- **D6**—Slides to the D position to support D4.
- **D3**—Slides back to the B position, and has the high-crease responsibility.
- **D2**—Holds at the A position, and has the low-crease responsibility.
- **D1**—Supports at the E position, and anticipates a pass to the wing area.

All are responsible for the diagonal pass.

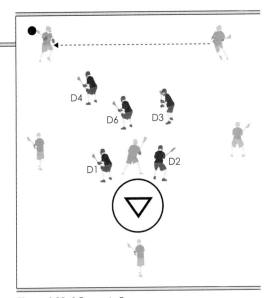

Figure 4.20 3 Passes to 5

5 Passes to 1

RESPONSIBILITIES
- **D1**—Picks up the ball at the wing area.
- **D4**—Slides back to the D area quickly.
- **D6**—Drops down to the E position, supports D1, and anticipates a pass to point behind.
- **D2**—Supports the crease at the A position.
- **D3**—Faces the ball at the B position.

All are responsible for a diagonal pass.

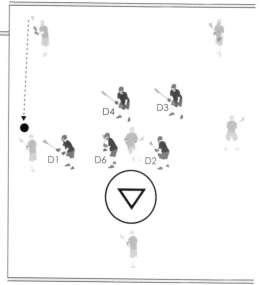

Figure 4.21 5 Passes to 1

1 Passes to Point (X)

Coverage 1. There is a concern that during the short instance, when D1 returns to replace D6 when the ball is passed behind, the onside area of the crease has no coverage. In this situation, the triangle technique (D3, D4, and D6) would be appropriate. The *offside middie (D3)*, or the middie away from the ball, would anticipate and fill for D6 on the diagonal slide. This would leave D2 at the A position. This move would also protect the crease area until D1 returns. At this time, D3 would rotate back up front to a position next to D4.

Figure 4.22 1 Passes to Point (X)

RESPONSIBILITIES

- **D6**—Employs the one-behind principle.
- **D1**—Must get back quickly to give support on the near side crease.
- **D2**—Holds at the A position; is responsible for the crease and anticipates a pass to the 2 wing.
- **D3**—Slides to the X position, and anticipates a feed to the crease.
- **D4**—Supports at the C position, and is responsible for the first pass out front.
  - If the first pass goes to the 3 position, D4 covers 3 and D3 rotates up to cover the 5 position.
  - If the first pass goes to the 5 position, D4 covers 5 and D3 rotates up to cover the 3 position.

Point Passes to 2

RESPONSIBILITIES

- **D6**—Returns to the crease on the ball side.
- **D2**—Picks up the ball.
- **D1**—Plays the E position, and supports the crease.
- **D4**—Slides to the B position, supports the high post, and anticipates a pass to the 3 position.
- **D3**—Anticipates a pass to the 2 wing, and fills for D4 at the D position.

Figure 4.23 Point Passes to 2

2 Passes to 3

RESPONSIBILITIES

- **D4**—Picks up the ball.
- **D3**—Supports at the D position, and is responsible for the high post.
- **D2**—Returns quickly to the A position.
- **D6**—Plays a high-crease position.
- **D1**—Supports at the E position.

At this time the defense has completed a full rotation. The only people in different positions are D4 and D3.

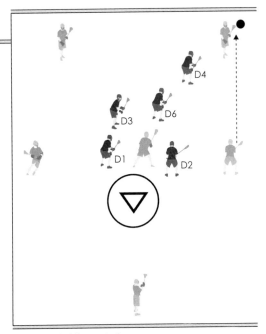

Figure 4.24 2 Passes to 3

Coverage 2. Coverage 2 would be identical to coverage 1 with the exception of when the ball gets to point behind. At this time, the coverage would be a complete five-man rotation.

Once the players are familiar with the four-man and the five-man zones and are totally aware of their responsibilities, then it would be appropriate to teach the six-man zone packages.

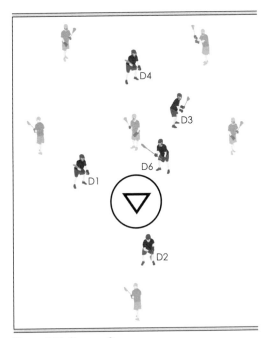

Figure 4.25 Coverage 2

Black Defense

Double Backer vs. 2-1-3 (Basic)

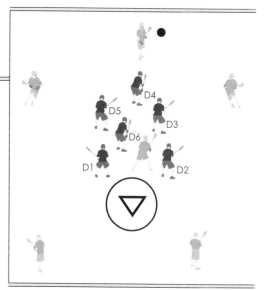

With the ball starting at the 4 position, the defensive players would be stationed in a double-triangle look.

RESPONSIBILITIES
- **D4**—Covers the ball.
- **D3**—Supports in the B position.
- **D5**—Supports in the D position.
- **D6**—Plays a high-crease position.
- **D1**—Supports at the E position.
- **D2**—Supports at the A position.

Figure 4.26 Black Defense, Double Backer vs. 2-1-3 (Basic)

The backer position would be either D3 or D5, depending on which side 4 attacks.

Assuming 4 forces to the left, D3 would be the backer, and D5 supports at the C position. Likewise, if 4 should force to the right, D5 would be the backer, and D3 would support at the C position.

4 Passes to 5

RESPONSIBILITIES

- **D5**—Picks up the ball.
- **D4**—Recovers to D5's position at the D position.
- **D3**—Supports the B position.
- **D6**—Supports the high-crease area.
- **D1**—Supports the E position, and anticipates a pass to the 1 position.
- **D2**—Supports the A position.

Primary backer is D4.

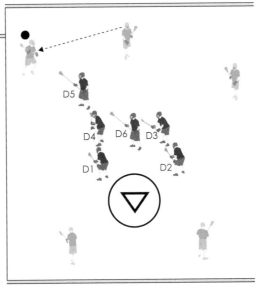

Figure 4.27 4 Passes to 5

5 Passes to 1

RESPONSIBILITIES

- **D1**—Picks up the ball.
- **D6**—Slides to the E position, and becomes the primary backer.
- **D4**—Quickly drops to the E+ position, and supports D6 if he must go.
- **D5**—Slides to the D position.
- **D2**—Supports at the X position, and watches the crease.
- **D3**—Slides to the A+ position, and also supports the crease.

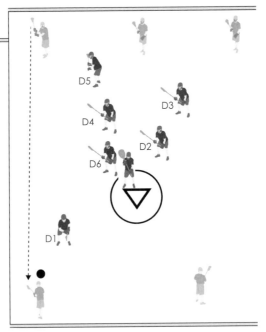

Figure 4.28 5 Passes to 1

1 Passes to 2

At this time, the zone becomes slightly vulnerable, and every precaution must be made to protect its integrity. Therefore, as 1 passes to 2, D6 must slide quickly across the crease to the A position, supporting D2 as the backer. The E position is temporarily open until D1 can get back to support. It is now the responsibility of D4 to secure the E position until released by D1. At that time D4 bumps back up to the A+ position that is being covered by D3.

COACHING POINT *It is highly important that this phase of rotation is practiced often, so it becomes a physical reaction for the defensive players.*

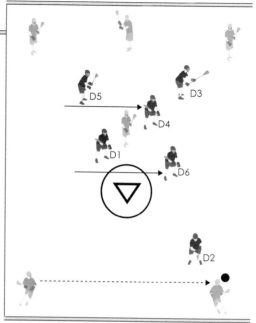

Figure 4.29 1 Passes to 2

RESPONSIBILITIES

- **D2**—Picks up the ball.
- **D1**—Quickly returns to the E position to relieve D6.
- **D6**—Slides across the crease to secure the A position as primary backer.
- **D4**—Slides to the E position, and when released by D1, bumps to the A+ position.
- **D3**—Secures the A+ position until bumped up to the B position by D4.
- **D5**—Holds at the E+ position, and reads the crease.

2 Passes to 3

RESPONSIBILITIES

- **D3**—Picks up the ball.
- **D2**—Quickly returns to the A position.
- **D1**—Secures the E position, and watches the low crease.
- **D6**—Holds at the high-crease position, ball side.
- **D4**—Supports the ball, as the backer, at the B position.
- **D5**—Supports the ball at the D position.

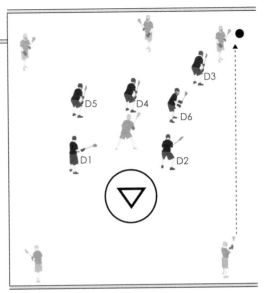

Figure 4.30 2 Passes to 3

3 Passes to 4

At this time, the ball has made one complete rotation and the defensive alignment has returned to the starting position as shown in Figure 4.31.

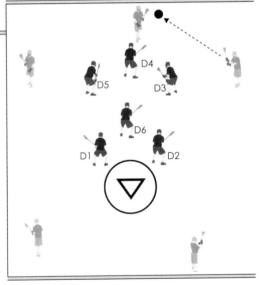

Figure 4.31 3 Passes to 4

Black vs. 1-3-2, Ball at the 3 Position

RESPONSIBILITIES

- **D3**—Picks up the ball.
- **D4**—Becomes the backer at the B position.
- **D5**—Supports the ball at the D position.
- **D6**—Holds at the high-crease position, ball side.
- **D2**—Supports at the A position, and helps on the crease.
- **D1**—Supports at the E position, and communicates with the crease.

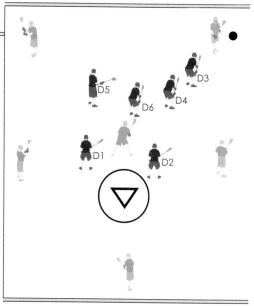

Figure 4.32 Black vs. 1-3-2, Ball at the 3 Position

3 Passes to 5

RESPONSIBILITIES

- **D5**—Picks up the ball.
- **D4**—Slides to the D position to support D5 as the backer.
- **D3**—Recovers to the B position, and helps on high crease.
- **D6**—Holds at the high-crease position, ball side.
- **D1**—Supports at the E position, and anticipates the next pass to the 4 wing.
- **D2**—Supports at the A position, and helps on the low crease.

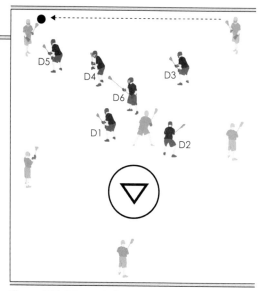

Figure 4.33 3 Passes to 5

5 Passes to 1 Wing

RESPONSIBILITIES

- **D1**—Picks up the ball.
- **D6**—Slides to the E position as the backer to D1.
- **D4**—Slides to the D+ position as the backer to D1.

COACHING POINT *If the 1 man at the 1 wing position attacks to the cage driving to his right, then D6 is the primary backer. If the 1 man at the 1 wing position attacks to the cage driving to his left, D4 would be the backer. The rule applied here would be the "under" or "over" call.*

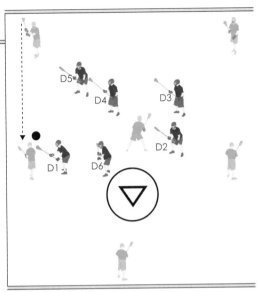

Figure 4.34 5 Passes to 1 Wing

- **D5**—Secures the D position, and slides to D+ if D4 becomes the backer.
- **D3**—Supports at the B position, conscious of the high crease.
- **D2**—Supports at the A position, conscious of the low crease.

COACHING POINT *D5 replaces D4 if D4 is the backer. D4 and D5 slide down and support at the E and E+ positions if D6 is the backer.*

1 Passes to Point

RESPONSIBILITIES

- **D6**—Picks up the ball.
- **D4**—Drops to the E position until released by D1, and then slides to the high X position.
- **D2**—Supports at the A position, and anticipates the next pass to 2 wing.
- **D1**—Quickly returns to the E position, and bumps D4 over and up.
- **D3**—Supports the crease from the B position.
- **D5**—Supports the crease from the D position.

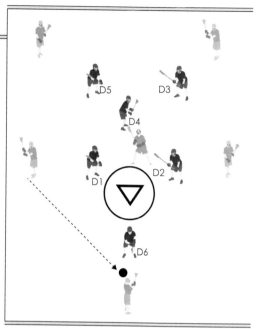

Figure 4.35 1 Passes to Point

Point Passes to 2

RESPONSIBILITIES

- **D2**—Picks up the ball.
- **D4**—Slides across the crease to the A position until D6 returns. D4 then bumps up to the A+ position, pushing D3 up to the B position.
- **D6**—Returns to the A position, and becomes the primary backer.
- **D3**—Holds the A+ position until bumped up to the B position.
- **D5**—Supports at the D position, and remains aware of high-post moves.
- **D1**—Supports at the E position, and remains aware of low-post activity.

COACHING POINT *The "over" or "under" rule applies here.*

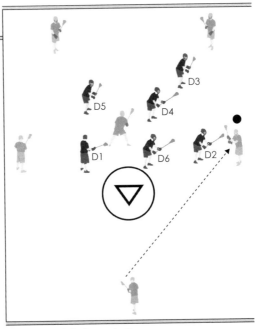

Figure 4.36 Point Passes to 2

2 Passes to 3

RESPONSIBILITIES

- **D3**—Picks up the ball.
- **D2**—Returns to the A position.
- **D6**—Rotates to a high-crease position.
- **D4**—Becomes the primary backer at the B position.
- **D5**—Secures the D position, and supports high-crease activity.
- **D1**—Supports from the E position, and remains aware of low-crease activity.

By this time, the ball has made one complete rotation, and the defensive alignment would have returned to the starting position as given in Diagram 4.37.

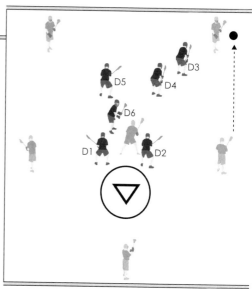

Figure 4.37 2 Passes to 3

Black vs. 1-4-1, Ball at the 4 Position

RESPONSIBILITIES

- **D5 (short-stick)**—Picks up the ball at the 4 position.
- **D3**—Supports at the B position, and is responsible for high-crease traffic as backer to his side.
- **D4**—Supports at the D position, and is responsible for high-crease traffic as backer to his side.
- **D6**—Supports at the high X position, and would support either D3 or D5 if either spot vacates.
- **D1**—Secures the E position, and anticipates a pass to the onside wing area.
- **D2**—Secures the A position, and anticipates a pass to the onside wing area.

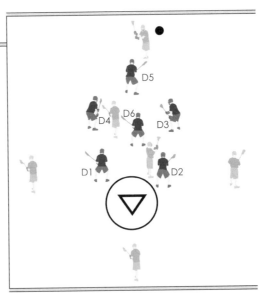

Figure 4.38 Black vs. 1-4-1, Ball at the 4 Position

The defensive formation will be the double triangle.

4 Passes to 1

RESPONSIBILITIES

- **D1**—Picks up the ball.
- **D6**—Slides to the E position vacated by D1, and becomes the primary backer if 5 drives to the cage to his right. This would involve the "under" call.
- **D4**—Slides to the D+ area, supports the crease, and becomes the backer if 5 drives to his left. This would involve the "over" call.
- **D5**—Slides to the D position, and gives high-crease support.
- **D3**—Supports from the B position, and remains aware of the high crease.
- **D2**—Supports from the A position, and remains aware of the low crease.

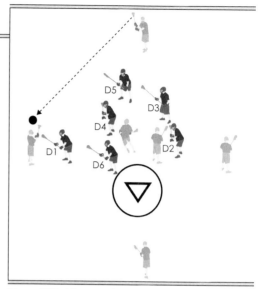

Figure 4.39 4 Passes to 1

COACHING POINT *When the ball is in the wing area on either side, the defensive alignment should be a 1-3-2 to the ball.*

1 Passes to Point

RESPONSIBILITIES

- **D6**—Picks up the ball.
- **D4**—Secures the E position until bumped by D1. D4 then slides to the X position.
- **D5**—Drops down to the E+ position. D5, D4, and D1 form a triangle around 4.
- **D2**—Holds at the A position, and would be the backer to pressure his side.
- **D1**—Quickly returns to the E position, supports D4 and D5, and becomes the backer to pressure his side.

COACHING POINT *When the ball is behind at point, the defensive alignment should be a 1-3-2 to the ball.*

Figure 4.40 1 Passes to Point

Alternate Coverage: Ball at Point vs. 1-4-1

RESPONSIBILITIES
- **D6**—Picks up the ball.
- **D4**—Drops to the crease, and covers the onside crease man.
- **D1**—Slides in to an outside E position.
- **D2**—Holds at the A position, and covers the onside crease man.
- **D3**—Slides out to an outside A position, and anticipates a pass to 2.
- **D5**—Covers the C position.

If 1 attempts to pressure to the right, the defense would employ the choke technique: D2 becomes the backer with D4 and D1 sliding to fill. D5 would hold and support the high crease while anticipating a pass to 3.

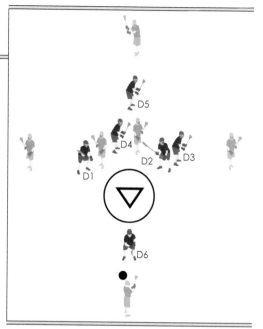

Figure 4.41 Alternate Coverage: Ball at Point vs. 1-4-1

Point Passes to 2 (Basic Coverage)

RESPONSIBILITIES

- **D2**—Picks up the ball.
- **D4**—Slides to the A position, and becomes the backer on "over" and "under" action.
- **D6**—Quickly returns to the A position, and bumps D4 up to the A+ position.
- **D3**—Secures the A+ position until bumped up to the B position by D4.
- **D5**—Holds at the C position, and anticipates a pass to 4.
- **D1**—Secures the E position, and watches the crease activity.

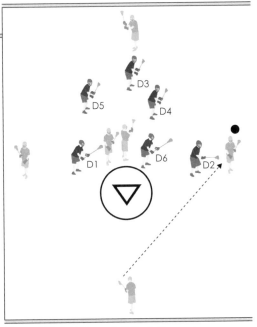

Figure 4.42 Point Passes to 2 (Basic Coverage)

2 Passes to 4

At this time, the ball has made one complete rotation and the defensive alignment has returned to the starting position as given in Figure 4.43. D4 makes a diagonal slide from the A+ position to the D position or bumps D3 across to the D position as he slides to the B position.

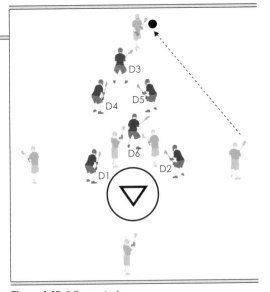

Figure 4.43 2 Passes to 4

Gold Defense (Five-Man Zone or Rover)

Familiarity quite often can be a detriment to a defensive philosophy. Without any coaching, players make natural adjustments to a defensive scheme that's been shown time and time again. To eliminate or alter these adjustments by the opposing offense, a team can apply a different defense and thereby cause havoc and partly dictate what offense will be run. The gold defense permits just that. It gives the defense an opportunity to aggressively pick away at the offense's feeling of confidence. It forces the offense to concentrate on the defense and change the offensive mode. Finally, it is easy to employ and fun to execute.

The regular five-man zone, used in the six-man zone and the man-down situation, would be applied here. The rules of the rover are as follows:

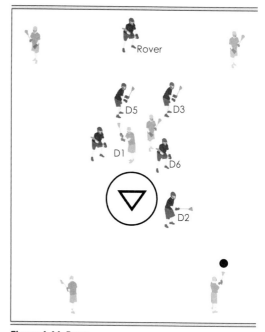

- Plays up top at the 4 position.
- Cuts off at the 4 position.
- Is positioned in front of or behind the 4 man.
- Can double quickly on the pass from the attack to the 3 or 5 middies (rover's discrepancy).

Figure 4.44 Rover

2 Passes to 3

RESPONSIBILITIES

- **D4, rover**—Reacts to the pass by forcing the 3 position as soon as he reads the pass being thrown by 2.
- **D3**—Anticipates the pass from 2, and rushes the 3 position with force.
- **D2**—Holds a strong support from the A position.
- **D1**—Supports from the E position, and must be alert of crease action.
- **D6**—Plays at the B position, and must be ready to react.
- **D5**—Supports the high-crease area, and anticipates a quick pass to 5.

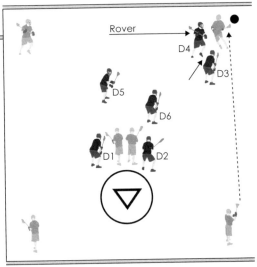

Figure 4.45 2 Passes to 3

Gold Behind

Rover plays behind at the point position.

- Cuts off at the point. Rover has the same responsibilities as he would have in the 4 position. He must be alert for any shots taken at the cage and react quickly to the ball going out of bounds.
- Positions himself in front of or behind the point man (1 behind).
- Doubles quickly on the pass from the middies to the 1 or 2 attackman (per rover's judgment). It is the responsibility of the rover to get to the back line first on any shots taken, to get possession.

Figure 4.46 Gold Behind

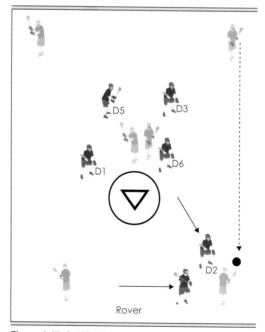

Figure 4.47 Gold Behind

Gold Number

Rover can now cut off a specific player at *any position*, at the discretion of the coach. If the player to be cut off is at the attack position and his number is 21, then the call would be "Gold 21." The same holds true for the midfield. The rover cuts off the numbered player.

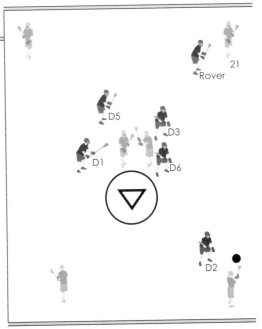

Figure 4.48 Gold Number

Sleeper

The gold defense can and has been played with the rover in a sleeper position. This is when the rover is situated at the midfield line and the defense plays a five-man zone. The attack plays back in a fast-break formation. Ironically, this formation places tremendous pressure on the offensive unit. It's on the offense's mind that if the ball is turned over on a shot or loose ball, the result could be an easy score. The easily applied gold defense is highly recommended to the team that is in a mismatch situation. It's a fun defense and builds the confidence of inexperienced players in a productive manner.

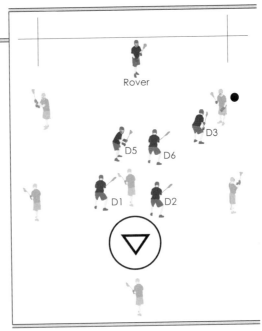

Figure 4.49 Sleeper

Matchup Zone

A highly effective zone, used quite a bit in contests by both colleges and high schools, is the matchup zone. Because of the adjacent slides, it is also known as the perimeter zone. It is quite easy to teach and can be used either in a full-time capacity or as a change-of-pace strategy. As the strategy of a zone is to force the opponents out of their game plan and to play a defensively determined style of lacrosse, this zone fits the charge. Basically, it is a four-and-two type of play with the short-sticks playing out front on the outside position or at the close, defensive wing positions. With the strong flavor of matching up that occurs in the game at the present time, the latter, with the middies back, seems to be more appropriate. Most teams are inverting the short-stick offensive middies and quite often, to protect the defensive short-sticks, it is beneficial to go to this zone.

Matchup: Basic Position—Front

RESPONSIBILITIES

- **D3**—Takes an inside-angle position, forcing the ball to his weak side. Force!
- **D4**—As primary backer, he must be available to attack the ball once the carrier decides to penetrate. Talks to the shorty.
- **D6**—Protects the high crease, and stays ready to be the secondary backer or the fill man for D2. Talks to D4.
- **D5**—Sluff-off covers his man and is available to support the middle if the ball comes that way. He drops down to support the high crease if the attacker goes down the farside.
- **D2**—Supports the right side of the crease. Takes the passing lane or stays in a position to cut off.
- **D1**—Supports the offside crease area. Talks with D6 and remains available to either slide across if needed or fill for D6.

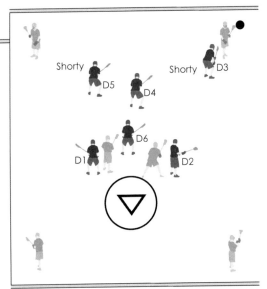

Figure 4.50 Matchup: Basic Position—Front

Matchup: Basic Position—Behind at 2

RESPONSIBILITIES

- **D2**—Takes the inside-angle position of attacker—must not be beat to the inside! Pressures the ball and anticipates that force is coming, by D3 to the outside and D1 on the inside.
- **D1**—Positioned at the center of the crease, he must be alert for any passes to the crease area. Becomes the primary backer if D2 gets beat to the inside.
- **D6**—Responsible for the onside crease if double crease, and for the man on the crease if single. D6 always faces upfield, looking for cutters, so he must listen to the goalie for the ball position.

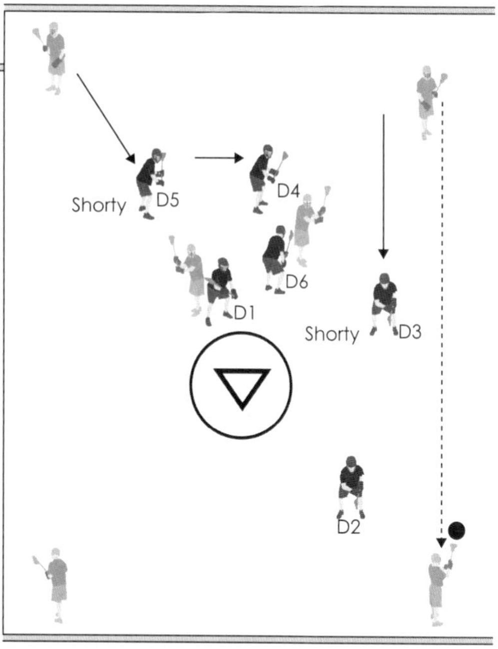

Figure 4.51 Matchup: Basic Position—Behind at 2

- **D4**—Best played by a long-stick. Positioned at the high-crease position, the B position, ball side. D4 must watch the eyes of the attacker and cut off any diagonal passes in the area. He fills for D3 if D3 goes to force
- **D3**—When attack to his side gets the ball, D3 slides to an advantage position to back up if needed. He is the primary backer.
- **D5**—Drops in to the high-offside-crease position. Reads the ball and adjusts. Drop to support the crease, if needed.

Matchup: Ball Behind at the 1 Position

RESPONSIBILITIES

- **D1**—Takes the inside-angle position of the attacker—must not be beat to the inside! Pressures the ball and anticipates that force is coming, by D5 to the outside and D2 on the inside.
- **D2**—Positioned at the center of crease. D2 must be alert of any passes to the crease area. He becomes the primary backer if D1 gets beat to the inside.
- **D6**—Responsible for the onside crease if double crease, and for the man on the crease if single. D6 always faces upfield looking for cutters and must listen to the goalie for ball position.
- **D4**—Best played by a long-stick. D4 is positioned ball side at the high-crease position, the D position. Must watch the eyes of the attacker, and cut off any diagonal passes in the area. He fills for D5 if D5 goes to force.
- **D5**—When attack to his side gets the ball, D5 slides to an advantage position to back up if needed. He is the primary backer.
- **D3**—Drops in to the high-offside-crease position. Reads the ball and adjusts; drops to support the crease if needed.

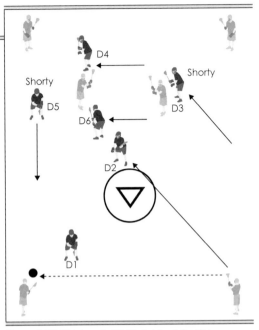

Figure 4.52 Matchup: Ball Behind at the 1 Position

The matchup zone can also be run with the shorty middies playing at the close defensemen's wing positions. The responsibilities would be exactly the same as for the wing defensemen. The wing defensemen then take the positions of the shorty middies.

Matchup: Basic Position—Front at 5

RESPONSIBILITIES

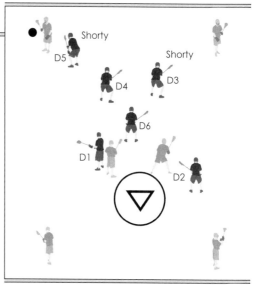

- **D5**—Takes an inside-angle position, forcing the ball to his weak side. Force!
- **D4**—As primary backer, is available to attack the ball once the carrier decides to penetrate. Talks to the shorty.
- **D6**—Protects the high crease and is ready to be the secondary backer or fill man for D1. Talks to D4.
- **D3**—Provides sluff-off coverage of his man and is available to support the middle if the ball comes that way. D3 drops down to support the high crease if the attacker goes down the farside.
- **D1**—Supports left side of crease. Remains in the passing lane or in a position to cut off.
- **D2**—Supports offside crease area. Talk with D6 and becomes available to either slide across, if needed, or fill for D6.

Figure 4.53 Matchup: Basic Position—Front at 5

Matchup: Shorty on the Defensive Wings, Ball at the 2 Position

The beauty of the matchup zone is the placement of the shorty midfielders. Besides playing the top 3 and 5 positions, they can be called on to play low, at the 1 and 2 wing defensive positions. With the advent of the inverting middie, this positioning could be advantageous for the defense. It also allows the defending team to place four long-sticks in a riding position.

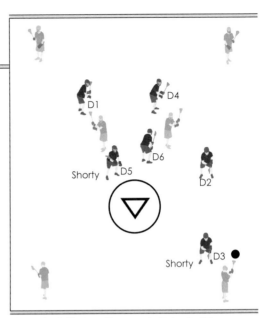

Figure 4.54 Matchup: Shorty on the Defensive Wings, Ball at 2

RESPONSIBILITIES

- **D3**—Takes the inside-angle position of the attacker. Must not be beat to the inside. Pressures the ball, and anticipates that force is coming by D2 to the outside and D5 on the inside.
- **D5**—Positioned at the center of the crease, D5 is alert of any passes to the crease area. Becomes primary backer if D3 gets beat to the inside.
- **D6**—Is responsible for the onside crease if double crease, and for the man on the crease if single. Always faces upfield looking for cutters. Must listen to goalie for ball position.
- **D4**—Best played by a long-stick. Positioned at the high-crease position, the B position, ball side.

Rover Defense

The rover defense is a single-backer-type zone defense that involves a combination of principles taken from the black defense, the matchup defense, and the old Hofstra zone. It's an exciting change in defense, easy to teach, and fun to play. Many have experienced the dedicated player who is tough as hell but lacks the stick maturity that is needed to play constantly. He is referred to as a "momentum" player, and can be used in the rover position with great success in this defensive scheme.

Rover vs. 2-2-2, Ball at the 3 Position

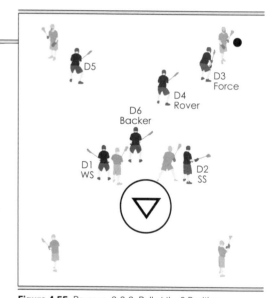

Figure 4.55 Rover vs. 2-2-2, Ball at the 3 Position

RESPONSIBILITIES

- **Rover**—Primary backer, both front and behind. Exception: he plays man-to-man coverage on a one- or three-front formation when the 4 position is covered. Basic position is at the C area.
- **D6**—Always covers the crease ball side. With the ball up top, D6 steps up to a high crease and is responsible for any action in his area. With the ball behind, D6 covers the crease and is responsible for cutters or ball-side crease players, always facing up field. Receives his information regarding ball position from the goalie.
- **D1** and **D2**—Play their respective positions, supporting the crease area and anticipating the next pass.
- **D3** and **D5**—Start at the front at cover or support positions. The support position should show a man-to-man technique.

Rover, Ball at the 2 Position

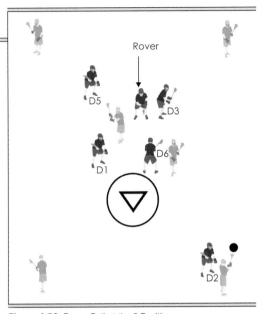

RESPONSIBILITIES

- **Rover (D4)**—Plays the high X position, and is available to back any penetration by 2.
- **D2**—Is responsible for the ball, and should play the outside-angle position.
- **D1**—Plays the E position, supports the offside crease, and should be aware of diagonal feeds.
- **D6**—Is responsible for any cuts to the ball side on a double crease, and plays man-to-man on a single crease, always facing upfield.
- **D3**—Plays the B position, and cuts off 3 if the rover doubles 2.
- **D5**—Is positioned at the D area and is responsible for diagonal passes. Fills for the rover covering the double.

Figure 4.56 Rover, Ball at the 2 Position

Rover vs. 1-3-2, Ball at Point

RESPONSIBILITIES

- **D1**—Assuming the ball is rotated clockwise from the 3 position, D1 would be responsible for coverage at point.
- **D2**—Takes a prerotated position at A+, playing in the passing lane of 1 and 3.
- **D3**—Positions at the high D area, concentrates on ball movement, and is responsible for 3 or 4, depending on ball movement.
- **D5**—Supports the crease at the E position, and anticipates the next pass on his side, playing in the passing lane of 1 and 5.
- **D6**—Assumes basic responsibility of ball-side crease coverage. Must communicate with the goalie.
- **Rover**—Supports the high crease, and assumes backer responsibility on movement, right or left, by 1.

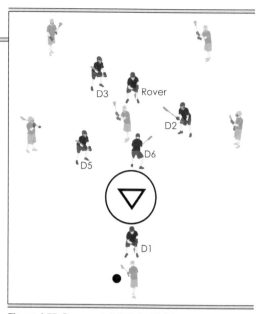

Figure 4.57 Rover vs. 1-3-2, Ball at Point

Rover: 1-4-1 Formation

An exception to the general rules of the rover defense is the 1-4-1 with the ball behind. Assuming D1 picks up the ball behind, the defensive formation should be one behind the crease, four across the crease, and one out front. Any backup slide would come from the offside crease, with the outside defender replacing the offside crease. In our terminology, this is a "choke 'em" call. The rover could rotate down to the crease, weak side, away from D6. He could also maintain his position and let D3 or D5 go to the crease. This is left to the discretion of the coach.

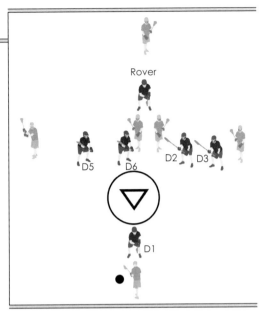

Figure 4.58 Rover: 1-4-1 Formation

RESPONSIBILITIES

- **D1**—Covers the ball at the point position, and harasses, but does not try to take it away. On any come-around moves, he receives support from the choke man (offside crease slide).
- **D2**—Supports the double crease at the A position, holds on come-arounds to his side, and is ready to choke on the force to the away side.
- **D6**—Supports the double crease at the E position, holds on come-arounds to his side, and is ready to choke on the force to the away side.
- **D3**—Covers the outside wing and supports inside.
- **D5**—Covers the outside wing and supports inside.
- **Rover**—Can drop to the crease, offside, or stay up top, supporting the high-crease area, showing respect to the 4 position.

Towson Tough Defense

Our defensive philosophy at Towson University became a reality more out of necessity than from the total plan. Our decision to implement defense as a priority in our game plan was made on a trip home from North Carolina State University a few years back. Both teams contributed to a score—29–19—that set a NCAA record in Division I lacrosse. Unfortunately, Towson was on the short end of that score. To this day, I still believe our goalie played a good game. A fact that attests to my feelings is that our goalie was carried off the field on the shoulders of over half of the celebrating North Carolina State team. Ironically, that year North Carolina State dropped lacrosse. That decision may have come about as a result of the electrical damage done to the scoreboard and the whiplash lawsuit brought on by their goalie. Since there has been a change in the athletic administration at North Carolina State, we will never know. On the bus trip home, my thoughts were concerned with the possibility of another such game, which surely would result in my hitchhiking north on I-95! I concluded that my chances for success in lacrosse came down to two options, a lobotomy or developing a defensive edge. I decided on the latter.

During the years when I coached a formidable Towson team, I often would contact the late Howdy Myers, when his great Hofstra team was in town for a contest, to discuss defensive philosophy. Though busy preparing an upcoming game plan, he always seemed to have time to answer and discuss any questions I had. The mere thought that he had the courage to be somewhat different always intrigued me. At that time I became interested in developing a defensive system with different fronts. Our decision to apply the multidefensive scheme rather than the traditional man-to-man was encouraged by the thought that the defense would be placed in an aggressive position, showing flexibility rather than the basic

127

man-to-man coverage. It was important that our defense be given an opportunity to compete with a variety of looks, which would force the opposing team to make adjustments in a short period of time, whether during the weekly practice or during the game. This would give us the defensive edge.

One phase of our multidefensive fronts is the tough defense, which basically is used as a secondary rather than a primary defense. It is not a front that a team might live and die with, but it offers an occasional different look.

Towson Tough Defense

The Towson tough defense is a sound front designed to give the opposition a different look while giving the defense an opportunity to accomplish the following goals:

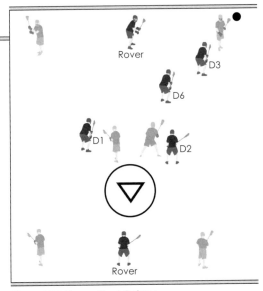

Figure 4.59 Towson Tough Defense

- Pressure the ball.
- Be in a position to back up.
- Take away individual play.
- Be in a position to control the ball after a shot.
- Afford the defense an awareness of the fast break.
- Force the offense out of its offensive strategy.
- Deny a pass to adjacent players.
- Award the double-team at any time.
- Eliminate designated offensive players.
- Force redirection on passes.

Like most defenses, the tough defense is a change-of-pace front and could be most effective if used as such. As my philosophy on defense dictates different looks to be successful,

the tough seems to blend in very smoothly. The following
illustrated breakdown assists with understanding the basic
principles applied to this defense:

TERMS

- Backer
- Force
- Strong-side support (SS)
- Weak-side support (WS)
- Rover point (RX)
- Rover 4 (R4)

To be as fundamentally sound as possible, it is best to start
the development of the tough defense working solely with the
inside *four defensemen*. Our basic formation is a triangle-and-
one to the ball, as shown in the following figures.

Triangle-and-One vs. 2-2-2, Ball at the 3 Position

RESPONSIBILITIES

- **D3, force**—Plays the ball one player position to the inside.
- **D6, backer**—Aligns himself between D3 and the goal, on an established arc, approximately five yards out front of the crease. He is the backer and supports the force man.
- **D2, onside support**—Plays a convenient wing position supporting the onside crease along with D6, and places himself in a position to cover the 2 area. If needed, he must be aware that if 3 passes to 2, D2 would then become the force man.
- **D1, weak-side support**—Gives backside support to the crease, but not in a flat manner. He must move upfield a few yards, staying in the diagonal passing lane between 3 and 1. He becomes the next rotation to pressure the ball on an onside pass (3 to 5). He should be aware *not* to get caught on a low crease.

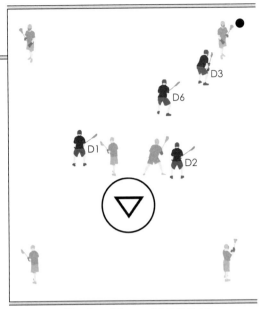

Figure 4.60 Triangle-and-One vs. 2-2-2, Ball at the 3 Position

3 Passes to 5

RESPONSIBILITIES

- **D3**—Drops into the crease area, becoming the weak-side support man, and assumes the same responsibilities D1 had when 3 had the ball.
- **D1**—Becomes the force, and quickly slides out to cover 5.
- **D6**—As the backer, D6 slides from the B position to the D position, assuming the same responsibilities.
- **D2**—Slides across the crease and again becomes the onside support man playing in the exact manner as when 3 had the ball.

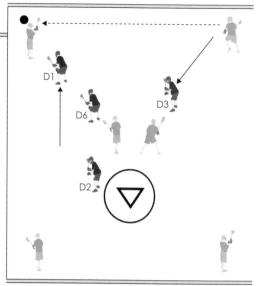

Figure 4.61 3 Passes to 5

5 Passes to 1

RESPONSIBILITIES

- **D2**—Moves from onside support to the force position when 1 receives the ball from 5.
- **D6**—Moves from the D position to the E backer position, being ready to back up and also being totally aware of the vulnerability of feeds to his area.
- **D1**—Converts from the force man at 5 to onside support, approximately at the E position vacated by D6.
- **D3**—Plays a weak-side support position. D3 drops down to the offside pipe proximity, and like D6, he must be cognizant of the vulnerability of his area for feeds. He should also play in the offside passing-lane position.

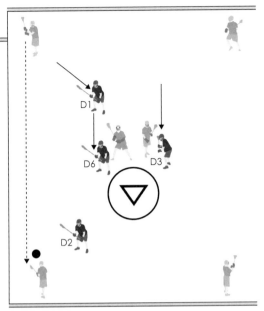

Figure 4.62 5 Passes to 1

1 Passes to 2

RESPONSIBILITIES

- **D3**—Goes from the offside support area to the force at the 2 position.
- **D2**—Becomes the offside man, playing basically the same position as D3 but at the E position.
- **D6**—Slides from the E position across the crease to the A backer position, keeping in mind the importance of his onside crease responsibilities.
- **D1**—Slides from the D support position over to the B support position, being aware of cutters and anticipating a pass from 2 to 3.

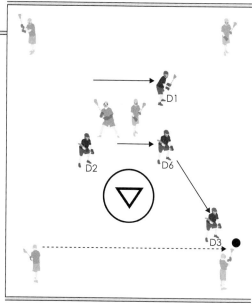

Figure 4.63 1 Passes to 2

2 Passes to 3

RESPONSIBILITIES

- **D1**—Becomes the force man at the 3 position.
- **D6**—Slides from the backer A position to the backer B position.
- **D2**—Becomes offside support going from offside pipe to D proximity.
- **D3**—Goes from the force at the 2 position to onside support.

As the triangle-and-one has completed a full rotation vs. the 2-2-2, the responsibility remains the same for all defensive players if ball movement continues.

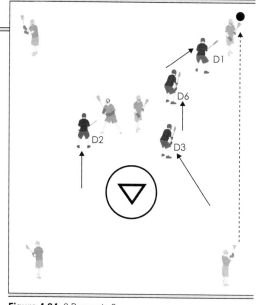

Figure 4.64 2 Passes to 3

The Triangle-and-One Defense vs. the 2-1-3 Offense

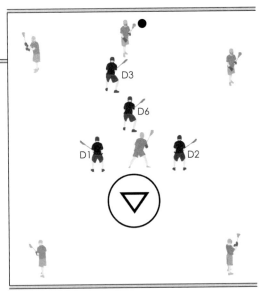

RESPONSIBILITIES

- The triangle-and-one defense remains the same vs. the 2-1-3 offense. The 4 player does not change the defensive strategy, because of the support of the rover 4 man who plays that any number of ways.
- **D6**—Changes his backer position to a C position when 4 has the ball.
- **D2** and **D1**—Balance out while D3 has an opportunity to anticipate his next move.

Figure 4.65 The Triangle-and-One Defense vs. the 2-1-3 Offense

The Triangle-and-One Defense vs. the 1-3-2 Formation

RESPONSIBILITIES

The triangle-and-one coverage is identical to the same coverage vs. a 2-1-3 and 2-2-2 formation while the ball is out front at the 3 and 4 areas. There is a slight alteration when the ball is passed from the 3 position to the 2 position:

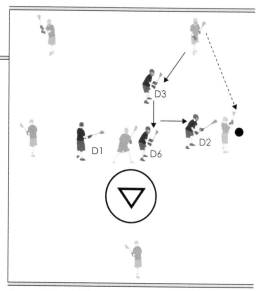

- **D2**—Becomes the force man.
- **D6**—Drops to an A position and _must_ be aware of the vulnerability to his left if 6 should pop out.
- **D3**—Drops in as quickly as possible to support D6, cutting off the high post and pop-out move.
- **D1**—Supports from the offside wing area, should not be flat, and must support the crease.

Figure 4.66 The Triangle-and-One Defense vs. the 1-3-2 Formation

2 Passes to Point

RESPONSIBILITIES

The one-man-behind principle is as follows: any time only one player is behind the
goal at point, the crease backer is called on
to play the force position to maintain balance in the total defense. Every defensive
player must be totally aware that this is a
time of transition when the defense can be
vulnerable.

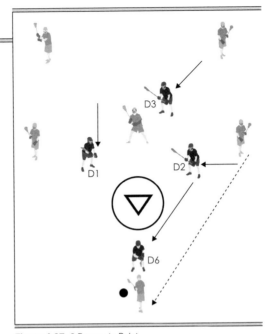

Figure 4.67 2 Passes to Point

- **D6**—Becomes the force at the point position in a 1-3-2 or 1-4-1 formation. D6
  should play the ball and not think "take
  away," but should harass, read eyes, and
  try to block any passes.
- **D2**—Once the pass is made, D2 must give
  a supreme effort to get back in to support
  the crease.
- **D1**—D1 plays an offside crease position, supporting inside
  out.
- **D3**—Because of the void left by D6, D3 must eliminate
  any threat to the onside crease. D3 must drive hard to the
  crease, and when D2 has returned to support (and only
  when he returns), D3 slides out to a high-crease area.

It is important to mention at this time that the defense
depends on the goalie to support the middle crease area by
placing his stick in a high position, helping to discourage any
passes to that area.

The Triangle-and-One vs. the 1-4-1 Formation

RESPONSIBILITIES

The one-man-behind principle applies here also. The ball starts at the 4 position. D3 becomes the force man, plays good position, and does not try to overplay. It is important to remember that balance is needed here.

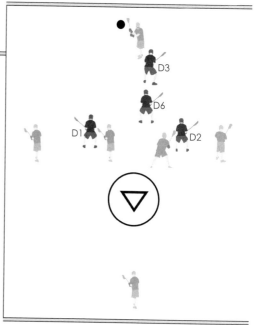

Figure 4.68 The Triangle-and-One vs. the 1-4-1 Formation

4 Passes to 1 Wing

RESPONSIBILITIES

- **D1**—Slides to 1 and becomes the force man. He doesn't overplay and anticipate the next pass.
- **D6**—Drops in to the E backer position being aware of the crease and pop-outs. He must always anticipate the next pass.
- **D3**—Moves quickly to the onside high-post position, supporting the crease with D6.
- **D2**—Gives offside crease support.

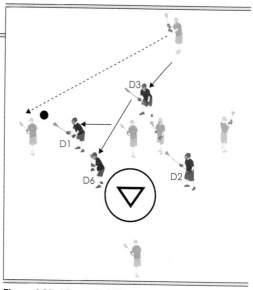

Figure 4.69 4 Passes to 1 Wing

1 Wing Passes to Point

RESPONSIBILITIES

All defensemen should support the crease and then balance out.

- **D2**—Holds the offside crease position.
- **D3**—Holds the offside crease position. D3 drives hard to the area vacated by D6, and once D1 returns, D3 should balance out.
- **D1**—Gets back to the crease quickly to release D3.
- **D6**—Slides from the E backer to the force behind at point, reading the offense all the way.
- **Goalie**—The goalie should again hold his stick high, trying to discourage all passes to the crease.

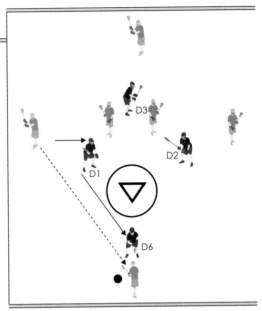

Figure 4.70 1 Wing Passes to Point

Point Passes to 2

RESPONSIBILITIES

It is vital to have support on the crease at this time.

- **D2**—Slides to cover 2. He must be alert to help discourage any feeds or passes to the crease, especially the high-crease area.
- **D3**—Must support the onside crease from the inside out. He slides up when D6 has returned.
- **D6**—Moves quickly to an A backer position, onside.
- **D1**—Should support the offside crease.

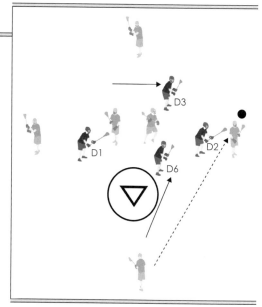

Figure 4.71 Point Passes to 2

2 Passes to 4

RESPONSIBILITIES

- **D3**—Becomes the force man, while the support people and backer align in the previously stated position.
- **D6**—Slides up to a support position at the C position.
- **D2**—Returns to his position at the A area.
- **D1**—Stationed at the opposite side of D2 at the E position.

This completes the rotation.

To introduce the tough defense, coaches may employ the four-man rotation of their choice. That's the beauty of the defense: you are not locked into any given standard.

One thing is certain: the tough defense can be confusing to play against.

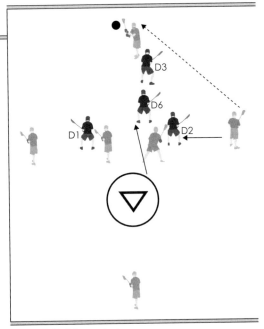

Figure 4.72 2 Passes to 4

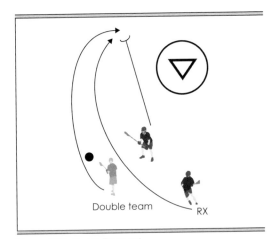

Figure 4.73 Double-Team at 1

Rover X (RX) and Rover 4 (R4) Responsibilities

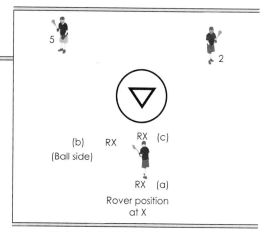

Figure 4.74 Rover's Position Behind

- **RX**—On a tough-regular vs. two-men-behind, RX plays a position between the two attackmen. He is to discourage passing between the two players and must be aware that he is to back up on any shots. RX is given the freedom to double-team anytime he feels the opportunity is available. When 1 drives to the goal without being in a position to see RX, RX becomes available to double-team. He also is in a position to double or to deny either attackman the ball on an "alert" call. He has the authority to call off the force man when the ball is being passed behind. RX vs. one-man-behind aligns himself in a position of advantage either in front of, behind, or to the onside of the one-behind. He again (a) is responsible for ball control on a shot, (b) denies the ball to the attackman at point, and (c) is given the freedom to double if the situation deems it necessary.

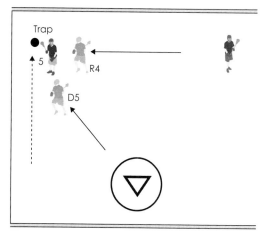

Figure 4.75 1 Passes to 5—Trap

- **R4**—R4's responsibilities are almost identical in the front position. On a two-front, he stations himself between the two middies. He also tries to discourage passes across the front and is given the opportunity to double when he sees fit. On any shot, he releases quickly to initiate the fast break. On an "alert" call, R4 can assist in doubling or denying.

Both RX and R4 are in a position to place tremendous strain on opposing players while affording their defense an opportunity to place themselves in a comfortable defensive scheme.

When applying the tough defense in total, the progression that seems most effective is to defend first the 2-2-2 offense with both rovers in their primary positions. It is important that the triangle-and-one develop a feeling of confidence and assurance at this time. In this way, the triangle-and-one and both RX and R4 are in a position to see how they can support each other immediately by means of communication. Also at this time, they work together as a unit and search for the proper timing needed in execution. Once they have become familiar with their responsibilities, you would advance to the 1-3-2 formation and explain how the force man, responsible for the 1 point-man behind, could:

- Be released of his force duties, balance out, and give support to the crease
- Double-team
- Use the face technique—for example, the backer relinquishes his basic responsibilities to another player and "face-guards" the offensive player(s) on the onside crease

Only when your personnel feel comfortable with their execution is it proper to use the 1-4-1 formation. This formation includes the R4, who also has the opportunity to execute in the same manner as RX did with the one-behind.

The Towson tough defense, as stated before, is a change-of-pace front that can be a lot of fun for players, giving the defense a commanding edge in gaining momentum, along with placing them in a position of defensive control.

Man-Down Defense

5

ONE OF THE JOYS OF COACHING WAS THE opportunity to have my sons Keith, Carl, and Curtis travel with the team to away contests. It was to be a positive and memorable experience for the boys, one that would contribute to the development of their attitude and values. Curtis, the youngest of the three and approximately four years old, was blessed with an outgoing personality. In a crowd, he seemed to blossom as the central figure of discussion and entertainment. One time, the players locked him in a locker while they dressed and prepared for practice. Another time, the campus police asked me to come to the student union immediately. They wanted direction as to how they should attempt to remove his arm from the vending machine. It seems the players coached the youngster to put his whole arm up the vending machine to try to get free drinks.

We were on our way home from Delaware on a bus when in the back of the bus Curt started to yell, "Oh, that's bad! I'm going to tell my daddy!" I knew then that maybe bringing the

143

boys on the bus was not a good idea, because it didn't allow the players the verbal freedom they needed—especially with Curtis around. He came down the aisle and started to yell that a player in the back had made a bad sign with his finger. There are times when as a coach you don't want to acknowledge some things that the players do. This was one of those times. But he wouldn't stop until I addressed the situation.

After finding out from Curtis who the culprit was, I told the player I wanted to meet with him in my office when we got to Towson. The player later told me that he had been talking with another player across the aisle and had given him the finger. He said he was unaware that the youngster was observing. I told him that Curt was a hearing-impaired youngster and was very observant. He and the other player would have to watch what they say or do when around the boy. He agreed, and we left it at that.

On the way out of the gym, holding Curtis's hand with my right hand, we passed by the admissions director, Mike Mahoney, and the player, Sam Pavola, both standing on my left, and bid each other good night. Approximately twenty years later, I met Sam Pavola and Mike Mahoney at an alumni function. As we talked about old times, Mike asked if I remembered that incident. I said I did. Mike asked if I remembered coming out of the gym holding Curtis's hand and saying good night to them as we passed by. I replied that I did.

Mike then told me, "As you passed by us, holding Curt's left hand, your cute little boy took his free hand, placed it behind his back, where you could not see it, and gave us the finger! Do you think this could have been an inherited trait from his mother's side?"

The Rotation and Zone Man-Down Defense

An exciting and challenging phase of lacrosse is the man-down defense. There are many different approaches to this segment of the game. A coach may go with the defensive unit on the field and simply replace certain positions, or he may use a special-unit approach where youngsters who don't have much opportunity to play are given the responsibility to defend. In this scenario, the defensive group quite often becomes highly cohesive, with the development of a significant personal pride and respect. This proactive approach has resulted many times in positive results. Whichever defensive philosophy is selected, the bottom line dictates that this phase of the game must be honored and given the appropriate respect in the practice schedule. Remember, the outcome of many games has been the result of a successful man-down defense.

One of the most basic defensive coverages applied in the man-down scheme is the rotation method. It is a very easy technique to learn for the man-down unit, but it requires an alert, anticipating mentality. All defenders must be on the same page as far as ball movement is concerned. The players must anticipate the next possible offensive option and when possible, prerotate to that position. Above all, *communication is vital!* Players should be barking out information about who has the ball, who is backer right and left, who has the cutters, and any change in the formation. The rotation defense can be implemented in two methods: (1) box-and-one and (2) the five-man rotation.

145

The Box-and-One vs. the 2-1-3, Ball at the 3 Position

RESPONSIBILITIES

- **D3**—Is responsible for the ball. D3 applies pressure, has to know he is covered, and anticipates the next move.
- **D5**—Is stationed at a C position, and tries to play between the ball and the 5 man. If the ball is passed to the 4 man, D5 plays the ball. If it is thrown to the 2 man behind, D5 turns, facing the pass, and moves down between the 4 man and the 5 man.

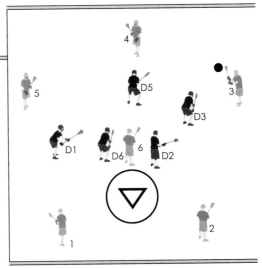

Figure 5.1 The Box-and-One Rotation vs. the 2-1-3, Ball at the 3 Position

- **D2**—Supports the ball from the 2 position. If the ball is thrown to the 2 man, D2 picks up the ball. On a pass to the 4 man, it is important that D2 hold the position until the next pass. A pass to the 5 man would alert D2 to slide across the crease, making him responsible for the 1 man on that side. This would be the first rotation.
- **D1**—As the farthest man from the ball, he is responsible for both 5 and 1, depending on the next pass.
- **D6**—Plays on the crease and plays strictly man-for-man until the formation changes to a double crease. At this time, the coverage on the crease should be a two-man zone.

Basically, the rotation principles are that the man on the ball pressures, both side adjacent men support the ball, and the farthest defender from the ball positions himself between the two opposing players farthest from the ball.

The defensive formation should always be a 1-3-1 set facing the ball.

The Box-and-One vs. the 2-1-3, Ball at the 4 Position

RESPONSIBILITIES

- **D5**—Has responsibility for the ball. D5 pressures under control and anticipates the next pass.
- **D3**—After a pass is made, D3 turns to the inside, always facing the ball, and drops down to approximately a B position.
- **D2**—Plays a basic position at the defensive 2 position, conscious of the next pass. If it goes to the 5 position, D2 must slide across the crease to replace D1.
- **D1**—As 4 receives the ball, D1 slides upfield, aware of staying in the passing lane between 4 and 1. He is responsible for 5 if 5 receives the ball.
- **D6**—Plays on the crease and plays strictly man-for-man until the formation changes to a double crease. At this time, the coverage on the crease should be a two-man zone.

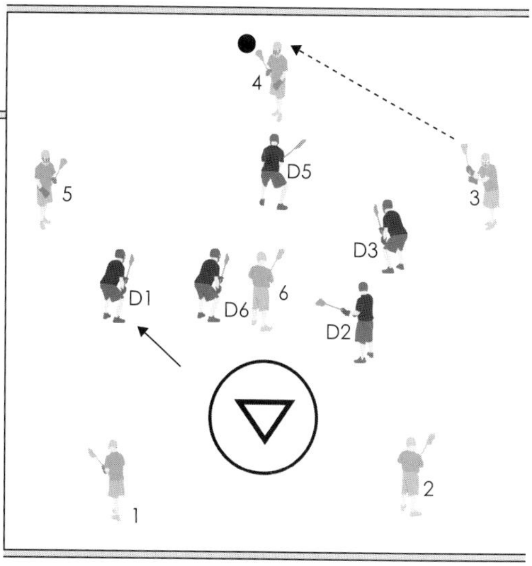

Figure 5.2 The Box-and-One vs. the 2-1-3, Ball at the 4 Position

The Box-and-One vs. the 2-1-3, Ball at the 5 Position

RESPONSIBILITIES

- **D1**—Slides out to play the ball, and harasses under control. If 5 passes to 1, D1 drops back toward the center, facing the ball.
- **D2**—As 4 passes to 5, D2 slides across the crease and becomes responsible for 1 if he should receive the ball.
- **D3**—Drops down to D2's basic position and becomes responsible for 2.
- **D5**—As 4 passes to 5, D5 drops down to the B position, always facing the ball. He must be in a position to cut off any passes to 3.
- **D6**—His duties are the same: plays man-to-man on 6.

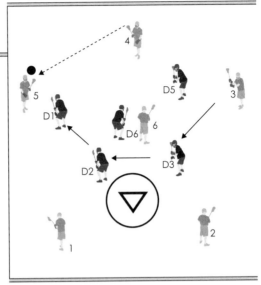

Figure 5.3 The Box-and-One vs. the 2-1-3, Ball at the 5 Position

The Box-and-One vs. the 2-1-3, Ball at the 1 Position

RESPONSIBILITIES

- **D1**—On the pass to 1, D1 should drop into the D position, his side, always facing the ball and anticipating a cutter to his side. He is responsible for cutters on his side.
- **D2**—As the pass is made to 1, D2 is responsible for covering 1 in a pressuring manner, hoping to interrupt any feeding possibility.
- **D3**—Drops down to the A position. Helps the crease and is responsible for 2 if 2 should get the ball.
- **D5**—He is stationed above D3 at the B position and is responsible for any diagonal passes on his side.
- **D6**—Plays man-to-man on 6.

At this time there has been a complete rotation.

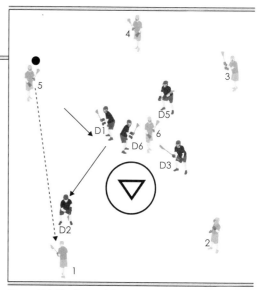

Figure 5.4 The Box-and-One vs. the 2-1-3, Ball at the 1 Position

The Box-and-One vs. the 1-3-2, Ball at the 5 Position

RESPONSIBILITIES

The responsibilities of the defense vs. the 1-3-2 formation are exactly the same as those against the 2-1-3, with the exception of a slight variation when the ball is behind at the point position. This is discussed when the ball is at that position.

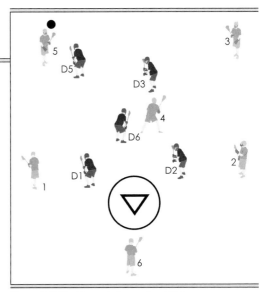

Figure 5.5 The Box-and-One vs. the 1-3-2, Ball at the 5 Position

- **D5**—Plays the ball in a pressuring manner. He must react quickly on passes to either side and remember that he then becomes a support player.
- **D1**—Positioned at the left side of the crease, the 1 area, D1 supports the ball on any drive and anticipates any directional pass made by 5.
- **D2**—Plays the offside crease position, the A position; must be alert to any diagonal pass to his side; and must be in constant contact with adjacent players.
- **D3**—Is positioned at a B position on the crease. He must anticipate the next pass, and as the adjacent player, he is aware of supporting D5.
- **D6**—Covers the man on the crease, and should help with communication.

The Box-and-One vs. the 1-3-2, Ball at the 1 Position

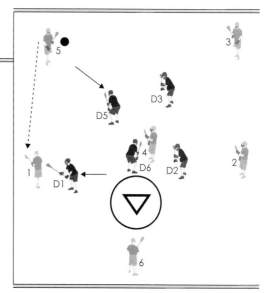

Figure 5.6 The Box-and-One vs. the 1-3-2, Ball at the 1 Position

RESPONSIBILITIES

- **D1**—Pressures the ball in a controlled manner, and anticipates the next pass.
- **D5**—After his man passes the ball, D5 drops in toward the middle, at the D position; supports the ball; and looks to help with intercepting any diagonal passes.
- **D3**—Plays a B position, and reads the situation. He must realize he is farthest from the ball and is responsible for 3 and 2.
- **D2**—Positioned at the offside crease area, the A area, D2 supports the ball and is responsible for the man behind, if that man gets the next pass or tries to come around.
- **D6**—Is responsible for man-to-man coverage on the crease.

The Box-and-One vs. the 1-3-2, Ball at Point Behind

RESPONSIBILITIES

- **D2**—Anticipating a pass to 2 from 6, D2 quickly goes behind to cover the ball, again pressuring this feeding position.
- **D1**—After the pass from 6, D1 turns quickly, facing the ball, and takes a support position at the E position. He should be alert to read the eyes of the behind attackman and help in blocking any feeds.
- **D3**—Has filled the vacated position by D2, becomes the support man on his side, and looks for any feeds to his side.
- **D5**—Rotates over to a center position, the C position, and is responsible for both 3 and 5.
- **D6**—Plays hard man-to-man at this time, since the ball is in a good feeding position.

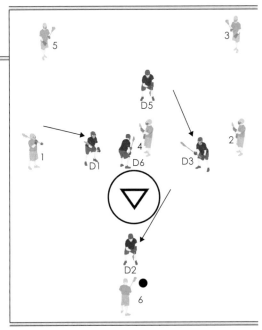

Figure 5.7 The Box-and-One vs. the 1-3-2, Ball at Point Behind

The Box-and-One vs. the 1-3-2, Ball at the 2 Position

RESPONSIBILITIES

- **D2**—On the pass to 2, D2 releases to the offside crease area, the E position, by way of the onside crease. He makes sure 6 doesn't attempt a come-around before he takes his proper position.
- **D3**—Pressures the ball, and anticipates the next pass.
- **D5**—Takes a position at the B area and supports D3, looking for any diagonal pass in his zone area.
- **D1**—Is the farside defender. Splits between 1 and 5, and is alert for any diagonal pass.
- **D6**—Plays man-to-man on 6, and gives verbal assistance to teammates.

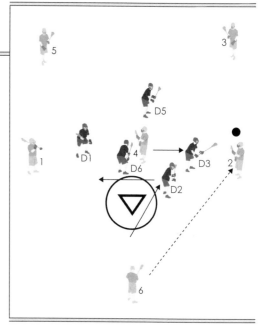

Figure 5.8 The Box-and-One vs. the 1-3-2, Ball at the 2 Position

The Box-and-One vs. the 1-3-2, Ball at the 3 Position

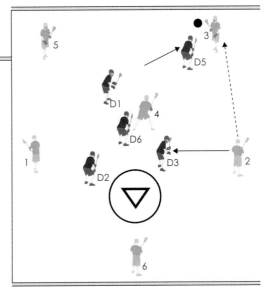

Figure 5.9 The Box-and-One vs. the 1-3-2, Ball at the 3 Position

RESPONSIBILITIES

- **D5**—Plays the ball in a pressuring manner. He must react quickly on passes to either side and remember he then becomes a support player.
- **D2**—Positioned at the left side of the crease, the 1 area, supports the ball on any drives and anticipates any directional pass made by 5.
- **D3**—Plays the onside crease position, the A position; must be alert to any diagonal pass to his side; and should be in constant contact with adjacent players.
- **D1**—Positioned at the C position in the center. He must anticipate the next pass, and as the adjacent player, he is aware of supporting D5.
- **D6**—Covers the man on the crease, and should help with communication.

At this time, the man-down defense has made a complete rotation with the understanding that *when the ball goes in one direction, the defense goes in the opposite direction*. When required to play man-down defense, the players are required to keep in mind the following important rules:

- Identify the formation.
- Communicate.
- Anticipate.
- React and rotate.

Man-Down Philosophy

As was explained earlier, the basis of all these defenses is constant, whether black, gold, tough, or man-down. The fundamental zone principles are used in the man-down situation; if and when strategy demands certain changes, those specific changes will be employed.

Vital considerations to be covered in the man-down preparation are formation tendencies and special situations. As certain formations were covered in the five-zone rotation, the following are explanations of three popular formations: the 3-3, the double-triple, and the 2-4.

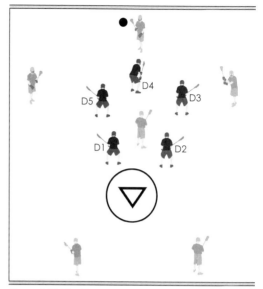

Figure 5.10 The Man-Down Philosophy

3-3 EMO vs. the Box-and-One, Ball at the 4 Position

A popular coverage used by many teams in contesting this specific formation has been the box-and-one defense. In this alignment D6 or D4, the short-stick, is required to cover the 4 position when the ball is out front and the crease, or the 6 position, when the ball is in the corners. This coverage has been referred to as "rope coverage."

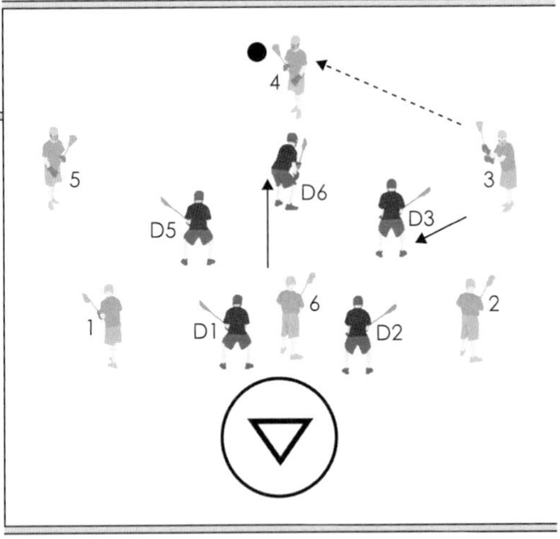

Figure 5.11 3-3 EMO vs. the Box-and-One, Ball at the 4 Position

RESPONSIBILITIES

- **D6 or D4**—Covers the ball at the 4 position on a pass to the 3 or 5 position, drops in to protect the crease and take away the diagonal to the corners, and has crease responsibility when the ball is at the corners.
- **D3**—Aware of the diagonal with the ball at the 4 position, picks up 3 if the ball is passed to that position.
- **D5**—Aware of the diagonal with the ball at the 4 position, picks up 5 if the ball is passed to that position.
- **D1**—Responsible for the diagonal to his side, and covers 1 if 1 receives the ball.
- **D2**—Responsible for the diagonal to his side, and covers 2 if 2 receives the ball.

All players support from inside out.

3-3 EMO vs. 1-3-1 (Diamond), Ball at the 4 Position

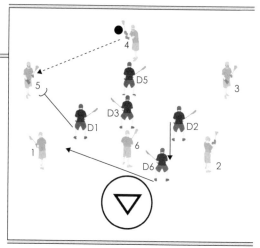

Figure 5.12 3-3 EMO vs. the 1-3-1 (Diamond), Ball at the 4 Position

RESPONSIBILITIES

- **D5**—Covers the ball, and on a pass to 3 or 5, D5 takes away the pass to the opposite front corner, either side, by playing in the passing lane.
- **D3**—Plays the C position, is aware of diagonals, and covers the crease when the ball moves down to the corners.
- **D1**—Positions himself between 4 and 1, takes away the diagonal, and is responsible for 5 if a pass is made to that position.
- **D2**—Positions himself between 4 and 2, takes away the diagonal, and is responsible for 3 if a pass is made to that position.
- **D6**—Supports the crease at the X position, slides to the side of ball, and is responsible for 1 and 2 if they get the ball.

All players support from inside out.

3-3 EMO vs. Umbrella (Cover 14)

The man-down defense I have accepted to contest the 3-3 is referred to as the umbrella coverage (cover 14). It meets all the specifics needed, is sound, and is easy to teach. It also permits the availability of cutoffs, adjacent denials, and constant pressure. The key in the coverage is that the crease is covered by a two-man inside zone. This two-man zone is responsible for the crease along with the 1 and 2 positions.

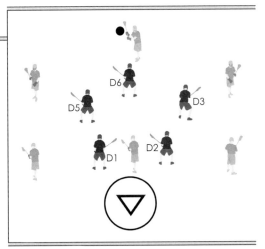

Figure 5.13 3-3 EMO vs. Umbrella (Cover 14)

RESPONSIBILITIES

- **D4 or D6**—Covers the ball at 4; on a pass to 3 or 5, he is positioned at the C position aware of the diagonal.
- **D3**—Plays in a passing lane between 4 and 2, and is responsible for 3 if he receives the ball.
- **D5**—Plays in a passing lane between 4 and 1, and is responsible for 5 if he receives the ball.
- **D2**—Splits the crease with D1, is responsible for 2 with ball on his side, and is responsible for the crease with ball at 1.
- **D1**—Splits the crease with D2, is responsible for 1 with ball on his side, and is responsible for the crease with ball at 2.

3-3 EMO vs. Umbrella, Ball at the 1 Position

When the ball reaches the down corners (1 or 2), the offside middie (D3 or D5) drops down to a passing lane between 1 and 2. At this time, D4 must get into the passing lane between the diagonals (2 and 5, 1 and 3). If a diagonal pass, 2 to 5, is made, D4 may play the ball and D1 would bump up, as would D5.

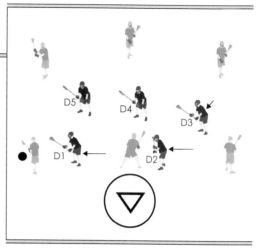

Figure 5.14 3-3 EMO vs. Umbrella, Ball at the 1 Position

Double-Triple

The attempt, in this coverage, is to play either a diamond-and-one up or a box-and-one down. This depends upon where the ball starts. If the ball starts up top at the 3 or 5 position, the formation should be the diamond with the extra man playing the ball. If the ball starts at the 1 or 2 position, the box-and-one would be applied with the extra man playing up top away from the ball, taking away the diagonal. Any cutters, in either formation, are the responsibility of the closest defender, with the next closest defender balancing up the defensive formation.

Double-Triple, Ball at the 3 Position

RESPONSIBILITIES

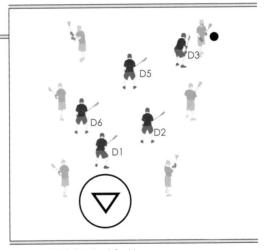

Figure 5.15 Ball at the 3 Position

- **D3**—Picks up the ball.
- **D5**—Stations himself at a high C position, takes away the diagonal to the 6 man, and anticipates the pass to the 5 man.
- **D2**—Plays at the A+ position, ready to attack 4 if he gets the ball; on a diagonal to the 1 man, D2 must drop fast to cover 2.
- **D6**—Plays at the X position, and is responsible for a pass to the 1 or 2 man.
- **D1**—Stationed between 1 and 6, anticipates a pass to the 6 man, may be called to cover the 1 man if the ball is by-passed to 2, and takes away the diagonal to the 1 man.

Double-Triple, Ball at the 2 Position

RESPONSIBILITIES

- **D2**—Plays the ball, and must harass the bottom hand, trying to force a bad shot or feed.
- **D1**—Is stationed at the E position, ready to back D2 if needed, and anticipates a pass to 1.
- **D3**—Is positioned to play 6, and should support middle coverage.
- **D6**—Is positioned at the D area, supports the diagonal, and is ready to slide down to the E area if needed.
- **D5**—Plays outside the box away from the ball above D6, and is responsible for the diagonal. On any cuts, D5 must be ready to balance the defensive formation.

Communication, as always, is vital in this situation.

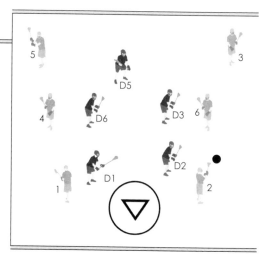

Figure 5.16 Double-Triple, Ball at the 2 Position

The 2-4 Formation, Ball at the 2 Position

The 2-4 is an EMO offensive formation that causes difficulty in the man-down situation. This formation places two players behind in the 1 and 2 positions as feeders, along with four across the crease, either stacked diagonally or stationed in a flat position. Because of the proximity to the goal, each attackman behind must be honored in order for this coverage to be successful. Certain parameters are highly important:

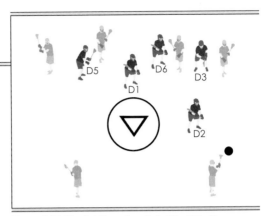

Figure 5.17 The 2-4 Formation, Ball at the 2 Position

- Never play between the stacks.
- Be aware of the soft and hard calls (play the man behind soft or hard, depending on the call).
- Pick up the ball only when released.
- When possible, zone the stacks ("dizzy" call).
- When possible, use the "choke 'em" technique.

Since this formation is very difficult to defend, it is imperative that all defenders communicate constantly, as at times the situation may demand a change in defensive play.

2-4 Stack, Ball at the 2 Position

RESPONSIBILITIES

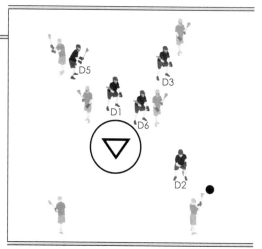

- **D2**—Always picks up the ball in the dead-ball situation on his side, plays soft, unless hard was called. On a pass to the 1 position, he must be sure to get back to the onside low post to release the choke-'em defender (man responsible for covering the ball).
- **D1**—Takes an inside position on the low stack, communicates on all picks, becomes the choke-'em defender when the ball is passed to the 1 position. He waits for the release from D6.

Figure 5.18 2-4 Stack, Ball at the 2 Position

- **D6**—Takes an inside position on the low stack, communicates on all picks, and zones with D3 when possible. Must remember that he is the choke-'em defender on the return pass to the 2 position.
- **D3**—Plays inside the high post and above D2. Zones with D2 whenever possible, and supports the low post when D2 becomes the choke-'em defender.
- **D5**—Plays inside the offside high post above D1, zones whenever possible, communicates on all picks, and supports the low post when D1 becomes the choke-'em defender.

2-4 Flat EMO vs. 2-3 Tight

To be effective in covering this particular EMO set, it is important to place the long-stick defenders (three) between the front four, as quick sliding is vital. The remaining two close defenders, one long-stick and one short-stick, are positioned on the crease slightly above the goal line. The long-stick should play on the side of the percentage feeder, while the short-stick defender plays on the opposite side. An important point to stress is that this set should never have both close defenders behind at the same time unless a "game" call has been made.

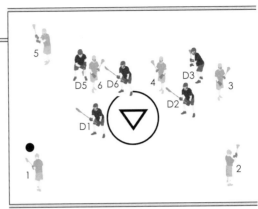

Figure 5.19 2-4 Flat EMO vs. 2-3 Tight

RESPONSIBILITIES

- **D1 (long-stick)**—Positioned on the crease above the goal line, picks up the ball in the soft zone. On a pass over to the 2 man, D1 must get back to his initial position, supporting the offside crease and taking away the diagonal to the 5 man.
- **D2 (short-stick)**—Positioned on the crease above the goal line offside, supports the crease, watches for the diagonal to the 2 man, and picks up the ball when released by D6.
- **D6**—Covers the onside crease position (6), and must anticipate the pass to the 2 position and slide accordingly to the other side to cover 4.
- **D5**—Supports inside with D6 and is cognizant of the outside man (5). On a pass to position 2, he must slide inside and support the offside crease until D1 returns.
- **D3**—Gives inside support on the offside crease, is cognizant of the outside man, and anticipates a pass to the 2 position. On the pass to the 2 position, he picks up the 3 man when released by D6.

Transition

A **FEW YEARS BACK I HAD THE OPPORTUNITY TO** speak at a coach's clinic in Syracuse, New York. My presentation involved the clearing game and how to approach it in practice. This was at a time when a lot of practice was spent on clearing and riding. Prior to the clinic I had an opportunity to visit with three of my ex-players who were coaching and in attendance. I asked each one to sit in a different area of the arena. I also mentioned that I was going to call on each one at a certain time during my lecture and ask them to tell me their responsibility on certain clears. At that time, they were to stand up and without hesitation, yell out, "Coach, on this clear I would start at the _____ position and quickly move to the _____ position!" I also gave each one an index card with a typed answer for them to read aloud.

While going through the presentation, I tried to emphasize the importance of this phase of the game, how significant it is that the players know exactly what to do, and how quickly it can be incorporated into the practice schedule. I actually had clinic players available to demonstrate all the clears and show how quickly these clears could be learned. I tried to emphasize to the coaches that it was worth the time, easy to do, and something that would stay with them. At this time, I called out asking if there were any ex-Towson players present. When the three hands went up, I exclaimed to the crowd that I didn't know they had come and that I wanted to prove a point. I called out to each ex-player individually to tell me exactly what he would do on the Mike clear, the red-d clear, and the alley clear. All three responded precisely as instructed, and we literally knocked the crowd over. They were totally impressed with my technique and sold on my philosophy. Ain't I something!

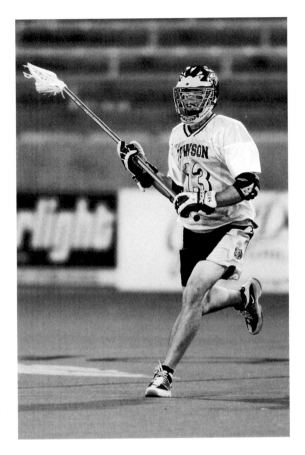

Approximately ten years later, Paul Wehrum, successful coach of Herkimer Community College and Hall of Fame member, was speaking at a clinic. Paul was a highly emotional coach who thrived on inspiration—from those around him, from written or spoken statements—and was driven to create a positive environment within his team. As he spoke on his topic, he paused for a moment to shed light on how impressed he was years back as he sat at a coaching clinic listening to "Coach Runk talk about his strategy in coaching." He was impressed by the response of the ex-players that day and how after all those years, they still remembered their assignments. He said this was a coaching strategy that he himself must adopt and apply to his program. I never had the heart to tell Paul that I was just joshing, and that just like any other coach, I struggled to get the little pencil-necks to do what I wanted. (Half the time they never did.) Paul, wherever you are, I hope you won't feel ill toward me for having fun again with the coaches!

Transition Offense

Fast-Break Box

Probably the most exciting phase of lacrosse, when performed correctly, is the fast break. The excitement created by an outstanding effort of the goalie with the outlet pass or a defender sweeping up a loose ball and moving it downfield, initiating the break, is overwhelming. A well-executed break can change the complexion of a game and give crushing momentum to the fast-break team. To be successful in this area, each offensive player must be totally aware of his responsibilities. Once this is accomplished, it wouldn't hurt to run the hell out of the fast-break drill in practice.

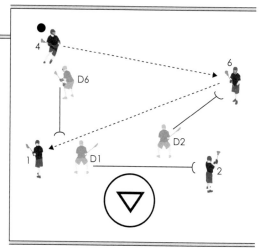

Figure 6.1 Fast-Break Box

RESPONSIBILITIES

- **4**—Comes down the field quickly preparing to pass the ball to the point man. He drives in with the ball until the point defender picks him up. Any pass before this happens causes an early rotation by the defense and lowers the success percentage. He keeps his stick at a twelve-o'clock position (vertical) when passing. This eliminates the poor-percentage pass and increases the chances for success. He must be aware that the three-o'clock position is a poor-percentage pass and should not be attempted. He must throw a strike to the stick of the point man whose stick is placed in the box position (head of the stick above the onside shoulder and head, at twelve o'clock). His second option is to look for the diagonal feed to 2, if 2 is available. His third option is to pass the ball to 1. Anytime he decides to throw the ball to the 1 man, he should drift about three slow steps to the center after the pass and sprint toward the ball for a feed and shot. This is referred to as a V-cut and is usually a good wrinkle with high percentage.

- **6, point man**—He is the quarterback of the fast break. He should be an athlete with good feeding skills and the ability to quickly read the situation. His position is approximately fifteen yards out, and he should be facing across the field with his stick in the box position (above his head and shoulder). He is responsible for calling any tricks or games. When receiving the ball, there should be only one quick cradle, followed by a pitched ball to the 1 man. The only defender the point man is concerned with is D6, the point defender. 6 must get the ball to the 1 man, who is cutting to the crease, before D6 can recover to the hole area. If at any time upon receiving the ball he is pressured by the rotating defender, D2, 6 will roll away from the poke check, drive toward the goal, and shoot.

- **1, attack (the diagonal)**—Should be a sufficient left-hander. However, if there are no left-handers, it would be appropriate to have the 1 man go with his strong hand instead of going with a weak left. 1 attack should play about eight yards out and four to five yards upfield. He must read the situation and on a pass to the point man, move quickly to the crease to receive the feed from the point. He must beat the point defender (D6). With a defense that plays shallow (out about twelve yards) and rotates quickly, it would be in his best interest, at times, to rotate upfield above coverage for the feed from the point man and the shot.

- **2, attack (low post)**—Stationed about eight yards out and four to five yards upfield. He should keep the outside foot upfield and the inside foot staggered. This enables a quick release for a shot if he receives the ball with good hip rotation. On receiving the ball from the point, his options are to (1) shoot, (2) feed across to the offside attack, or (3) look diagonally upfield for the fast-break middie.

Fast-Break Diamond

The diamond formation can be used effectively when the break is coming down the center or to the side the point man usually plays. The defense is forced to play a triangle formation with both close defenders, D1 and D2, having to honor the crease attackman (6). In doing so, the wing attackmen should look to be open for feeds. A quick pass by 4 to 1 or 2 forces the close defender to rotate quickly to the ball, leaving the farside attackman open. An example would be 2 receiving the ball and 6 sliding to the right, which forces D1 to rotate farther and leave a good feeding lane from 2 to 1.

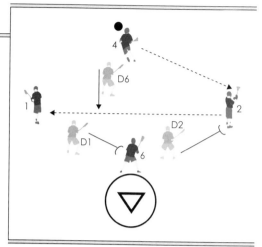

Figure 6.2 Fast-Break Diamond

Fast-Break Possibilities

Quite often, at all levels, it seems very difficult to execute the traditional fast-break offense because of the lack of certain player ability. At this time a coach may want to change strategies. The following changes have seen success.

Early. This call is used when the fast-break middie, 4, is five yards or so ahead of the closest defensive middie. The point man gives the "early" call, alerting the fast-break group that the ball, once caught by the point man, is returned to 4 for the power drive shot. Because of defensive strategy, the defense strongly tends to rotate on that first pass. This action leaves the 4 middie open and available.

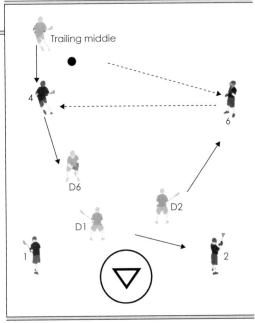

Figure 6.3 Fast-Break Possibilities, Early

Jack. An unsuspected wrinkle in fast-break strategy is the "Jack" call. At one time it was referred to as the "gotcha." The offensive team takes advantage of the situation because of the allegiance the defense has to their responsibilities regarding slides and who to cover on a pass in any direction. A coach will find this strategy fun to work with, as well as see a change in morale and momentum.

RESPONSIBILITIES

- **4, fast-break middie**—Drives hard to the goal, making sure to be picked up by the point defenseman (D6). At this time, 4 fires a strike to the point man and drifts down toward the goal.

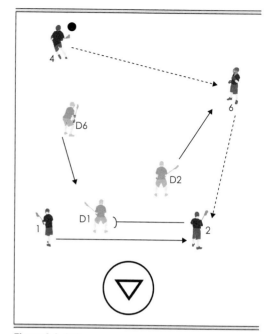

Figure 6.4 Jack

- **6, point man**—Alerted to the Jack call, plays a few yards higher than normal. This forces the sliding defender, D2, to go farther out to cover. 6 is patient and throws the ball to the 1 attackman when he has cleared the screen.
- **2**—Plays in close to the goal at the A position, and on the pass to 6, 2 screens D1. This should be an easy screen, as D6 already feels he has 2 covered.
- **1**—Plays in closer than normal. When 6 receives the ball, 1 cuts under the pick by 2. 1 should not be surprised as to how open he is, and places his shot accordingly.

Point

One of the "games" used in the fast-break mode is the "point" call. It can be very successful if all players are aware of the situation.

RESPONSIBILITIES

- **4, fast-break middie**—Drives hard to the goal, or forces the point defender to play him. His primary responsibility is to pass to the onside attackman, 1, and hold an outside position.
- **1, diagonal attackman**—Plays a little farther out than normal and is in position to receive the pass from 4. When in control of the ball, 1 creates a cushion to better feed the cutting point man.
- **2, low post**—Takes a normal position outside the cage, and on the pass from 4 to 1, 2 cuts hard to the outside crease area. This move should force D2 to react and give the cutting point man more room.
- **6, point man**—Hesitates, and as the defense begins to rotate, cuts hard to the goal, trying to find an alley or comfort zone to receive the feed and make the shot.

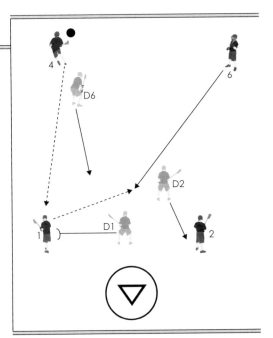

Figure 6.5 Point

Flat Break

One of the most unsuspected and high-percentage breaks is the flat break. It develops on the face-off or midfield loose-ball scenario. With the attack positioned in the restraining line area, the middie with the ball, 4, breaks toward the goal. It is important he *forces between 1 and 6*, trying to lure D6 to pick him up. This is the key! When it happens, he looks to get the ball to 6. Then 6 goes to the goal with the ball and must be aware of D2 making a slide to him. As this happens, 6 gives the ball to 2. Because D1 is responsible for sliding to 2 and is too far away, 2 should look to finish with a hard high-percentage shot. If he is covered by D1, which is highly unlikely, he tosses to 1 for the shot.

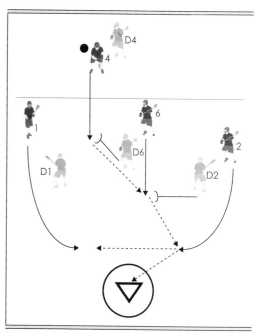

Figure 6.6 Flat Break

The flat break (or "catch 'em") is a great midfield break, but is unfortunately underused. Because the defense is drilled so often in the traditional break, this has the potential to catch them off guard. As an offensive weapon, it should be incorporated into the practice plan. You won't regret it!

Slow Break

Many times during transition in a game, the ball is brought downfield, not in a fast-break manner but in what is considered a slow break. This is one team with the ball coming downfield not having a four-on-three advantage, but in a situation where there is player advantage, such as a six-on-five or a five-on-four number of players. We have always referred to this as "more of us than them"! At this time, a green call is given by the players on the field or the bench. *Green* means "go to the goal." The players are given a flexible set of rules, detailed on the following pages.

Six-on-Five, Ball at the 4 Position

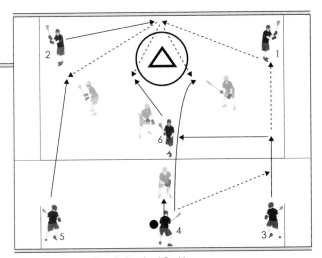

Figure 6.7 Six-on-Five, Ball at the 4 Position

RESPONSIBILITIES
- **4**—Brings the ball in until he draws attention by a defender. At this time he passes to the wing middie (in this case, 3) and continues in until the ball reaches the point position. 4 then cuts off of 6 to the open side of the crease, looking for a feed from the point man.
- **3**—Assuming he receives the ball from 4, 3 passes to the onside wing attackman and rotates to the 4 position in the middle, becoming the up-top shooter.
- **5, offside middie**—With the ball away from him, 5 continues down to the wing position and expects a pass from

174

point behind. If he doesn't have the shot, he transfers the
ball quickly to the 4 position.
- **6**—Plays up high about 10 to 12 yards, and cuts to the opposite side of the crease away from 4.
- **1**—If he receives the ball, he quickly transfers it to the point.
- **2**—He must cover the point behind when the ball is away
from him.

Note: this drill can also be run out of a 2-2-2 formation with
the diagonal middies, 3 and 5, cutting to the ball behind.

Five-on-Four, Ball at the 3 Position

On the five-on-four slow break, there are a number of tricks or "quick hitters" a coach can use to offensively attack the situation. It has been Towson's philosophy to first communicate the type of break available and then make the call. It is also beneficial to keep the five-on-four break looking somewhat identical to the six-on-five break so as not to confuse the players. The call for this scenario is "follow."

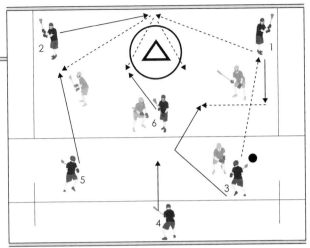

Figure 6.8 Five-on-Four, Ball at the 3 Position

- **3**—Brings the ball downfield, passes to 1, changes direction toward 6, in a slower pace to slow down his defender, and then explodes back out and toward the goal, looking for the feed from 1.
- **1**—Catches the ball from 3, and rolls upfield and toward the restraining line. He must be in a position to quick-feed 3 for the layup. If it is not there, he passes the ball to 2 at the point.
- **2**—After receiving the ball from 1, 2 immediately looks to the crease for the layup. If it is not there, he continues ball movement to 5 at the outside position.
- **5**—Continues to the wing position, and reads the situation. He is in a good position to take the shot after receiving the ball from 2.
- **4**—As a latecomer, he takes a position at the 4 area, up top. He should be ready to receive the ball from 5 and take the shot.
- **6**—Plays up high about 10 to 12 yards, and cuts to the opposite side of the crease away from 3.

Clearing Patterns

33 Post

33 post is an excellent clearing pattern from behind the crease or out of bounds. It is vital that D6 and D5 move down from the midfield about ten yards to eliminate the "bump." 4 and 3 play a post position and make themselves available to the ball. The stopper should look to 3 for the first pass. Anytime the ball is behind the goal, all players should move down ten yards toward it.

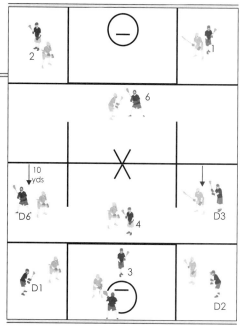

Figure 6.9 Clearing Patterns, 33 Post

43

The 43 is basically the same clear as the 33 with the exception that the low-post middie, 3, comes down alongside the goalie and positions himself to get the ball. If he is covered, he should automatically go into the crease area to receive the ball. Quite often, teams place their fastest man in this position. Again, all top players should drop down approximately ten yards.

Figure 6.10 43

Regular

The regular is a basic clear. If no call comes from the sideline, the players are aware to automatically go into a regular. D6 and player 5 are stationed in the alley. Either one is responsible for staying back, depending on the direction of the clear. 3 and 4 play between the restraining line and midfield line, approximately twelve yards apart. If the ball is thrown to D1 or D2, the onside middie drives to the ball, while the other runs an upfield diagonal to that side.

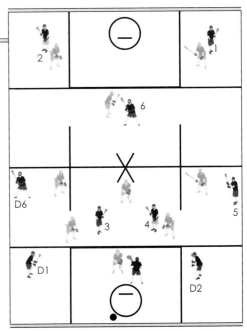

Figure 6.11 Regular

Regular-Deep

On the regular-deep call, the middies 3 and 4 are position between the midfield line and the far restraining line. A greater percentage of the time, they are covered man-to-man, leaving one middie available to cover two men on the offensive side. This should free up the wing defenseman and alley man on either side. It is also a good opportunity to execute the alley pass, one side to the other.

Rule: Anytime D6, riding 6 attackman, should bump up to ride, 6 must get into the clearing pattern, making him available in the clear.

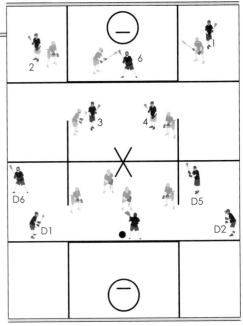

Figure 6.12 Regular-Deep

Mike

The Mike clear is a five-across clear with the middies to the outside of the close defenders. D6, or the "squirm" man, and player 5 are in a deep position on the other side of the midfield line. They should be covered man-to-man. This leaves four riders to cover five clearers. The clearing defenders next to the goalie should be approximately seven yards to the side and upfield five yards. The middies should be stationed in the wing area, five yards above the clearing defensemen.

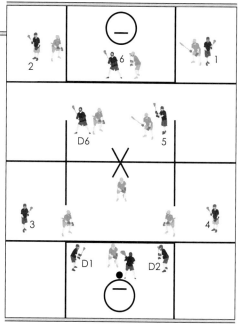

Figure 6.13 Mike

Regular Post

The regular-post clear is quite similar to the regular with the exception of the 3 man playing between the restraining line and the midfield line in the center. 4 is stationed in the center at a deep position. Both deep midfielder 4 and 3 must be covered, creating an adjustment with the riding attack that should force a two-on-one by the clearing team.

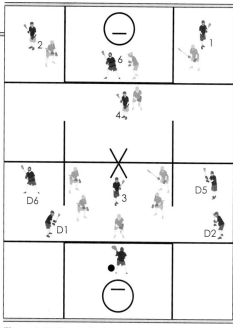

Figure 6.14 Regular Post

179

Stretch

The stretch clear is an excellent weapon for creating a quick four-on-three at the offensive end. The reason is the tendency for the riding team to leave the center riding middie right there—in the middle!

Note: 3 and 4 should be positioned at the wing line, giving the wing defensemen on both sides the visual ability to look straight downfield to the deep alley players.

Figure 6.15 Stretch

Alley

The alley clear is an attempt to place pressure on the riding team. It is best to sub D6 with the SS (short stick) middie, allowing four short-sticks on the clear. If successful, it can give the clearing team great momentum.

RESPONSIBILITIES

- **D6**—Takes a position approximately twelve yards deep in the offensive alley. If open, receives the ball, heads for the cage, and shoots or looks for the two-on-one. If D1 passes to the stopper or D2, D6 *sprints* to the midfield line, releasing 5.
- **D1**—First priority is to look for an open D6. If he is covered, looks to D2 for the diagonal

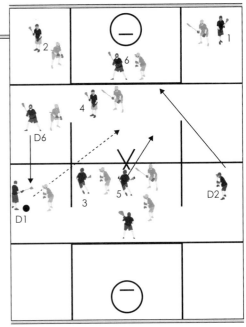

Figure 6.16 Alley

pass. If D2 is covered, D1 goes to the goalie, who attempts to pass to 5, breaking across and running a diagonal to the right.

- **5**—Must wait for D6 to cross over midfield before going over. If the goalie receives the ball, 5 gets open to receive a pass from the goalie.
- **3**—Plays at the wing or midfield area. Must wait for D2 to come back before going over.
- **4**—Should be positioned above the restraining line, ball side. Looks for the two-on-one.
- **Goalie**—Polices the defensive coverage. If he receives the ball, looks up for 5 on the diagonal.

Triangle

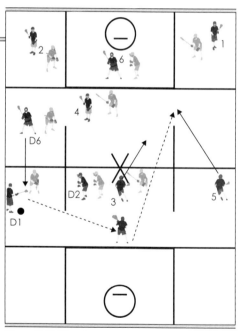

Figure 6.17 Triangle

The triangle is a midfield sideline clear quite similar to the alley. The exception is the defense is in a triangular formation on the ball side of the field. The advantage is the riding team must honor the two men over the line with midfielders, leaving the 3 and 5 middies to be covered by the remaining one defensive middie. The responsibilities are almost identical, as the clear is dependent upon D6 getting back over the line on the sound of the whistle. The cross-field pass can be made by either D1 or preferably, the goalie. This clear can be used as a quick break or a high-percentage clear, depending on the situation. It is the responsibility of the 3 or 5 to call out if he is the "hot" middie (not covered).

Sideline

The sideline clear is usually successful when executed just above the restraining line and below the penalty-box line. It can place the riding team in a very precarious position. Timing is very important in this clearing pattern.

RESPONSIBILITIES

- **D1**—Gives the ball to the middie at the sound of the whistle, and runs up to and out into the penalty box as close to the line as possible. This releases the SS middie ten yards away in the penalty box.
- **3**—After receiving the ball, 3 should curl to the sideline, looking to the SS for a quick hitter. After the pass, 3 sprints to the box, releasing D1 back into the game.
- **4**—Lines up in the onside alley. As soon as the whistle sounds, he *sprints* to the face-off area, calling for the ball. This action should also draw the covering defender to the midfield, leaving a large void area for the SS to run into uncovered.

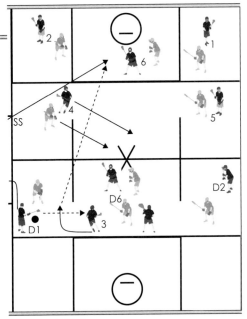

Figure 6.18 Sideline

Bringing the ball in on the sideline away from the penalty box doesn't change anything. The alignment is the same as it was on the penalty-box side, and timing is of utmost importance.

Note: sometimes passing the ball to the goalie gives D1 more time to get to the onside box area.

Gringo

The gringo clear is an offensive end clear with the ball just over the midfield line. The scenario could be one of two types.

Scenario 1: man-down-free clear with the ball being doubled.

RESPONSIBILITIES

- **3**—Takes ball, and on the whistle, turns quickly and tosses a pass to the goalie. 3 then runs back across the midline, which frees D2 to run the alley.
- **5**—Plays in front of 3 down by the restraining line. On the pass to D2, he stays and is ready to get involved if his man leaves.
- **D2**—Stays on the defensive end of the field until 3 comes over; goes across and toward the goal, looking for the pass from the stopper.
- **Goalie**—Gets in a good passing lane prior to start of game. Looks to pass to D2.

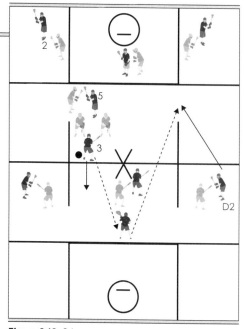

Figure 6.19 Gringo

Scenario 2: the cutoff. This occurs late in the game, in an all-even situation, with everyone cut off from the ball, and the best defender, takeaway player, covering the ball. Nothing changes, with 4 staying away from the alley side of the field.

Transition Defense

A very challenging situation in the transition game is the ability of the defensive group to work as a unit and discourage the fast break. The momentum that is achieved from a successful break can be devastating and presents a difficult time for the defense. Scores and momentum can change instantly in a contest with success in this area. A team scores and controls the following face-off, thus creating another scoring opportunity within seconds. Emphasis must be placed on working as a unit and using the proper technique to take the offense out of its pattern.

Many times in practice, defensive fast-break drills are set up at the restraining line with the 4 middie approaching from the midfield or the far restraining line. During this drill, the defense sprints back into the hole area and prepares to defend the break. Though this is appropriate for practice and occurs occasionally on the field, the emphasis should be placed on a more realistic situation.

More times than others, the defense is spread out somewhere near the midfield line, and this scenario should be emphasized in drills. During this period, it is vital that the players are encouraged to recover to the hole area and immediately form the defensive triangle, no farther than twelve yards out, facing the ball. They must also communicate with each other as to who has the point, covering the fast-break middie, and to not go out more than ten to twelve yards. Once they are all on the same page, they must anticipate and react in unison.

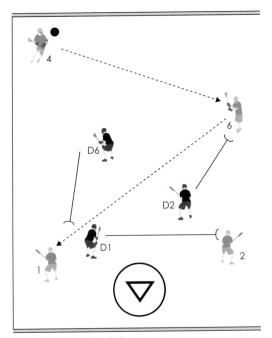

Figure 6.20 Transition Defense

Basic Rotation Fast Break

The obvious rule here is that the closest
defender to the ball becomes the point
man (the man responsible for picking up
the ball). However, for the purpose of this
explanation, D6 is the point man and D1
and D2 play their basic positions.

RESPONSIBILITIES

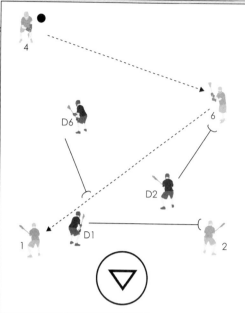

- **D6**—Makes the "I got the ball" call. He
  establishes a position approximately ten
  to twelve yards in front of the goal in a
  sound breakdown stance. Because of the
  overwhelming percentage related to the
  middie throwing the ball to the point
  attackman, we have always informed

Figure 6.21 Basic Rotation Fast Break

  our point defender to keep the inside leg
  back toward the goal. The reason is so D6
  does not have to take an extra step, since the ball usually
  is going to 6 at the point and D6 must turn, facing the ball,
  and run to the hole. By throwing his stick from a front position to a hole position in a quick manner, he increases his
  movement.
- **D1**—Plays at the E position on the crease, usually no farther
  out than the crease line. He must read the eyes of the middie and anticipate ball direction. Playing too close to the
  center of the crease will encourage a diagonal pass from 6
  to 1. This is eliminated by D1 staying home. If the pass is
  made to 2, D1 should slide across the crease quickly to force
  2. It is important that D1 read eyes and anticipate direction.
- **D2**—Positioned at a high wing position, A+, D2 must be
  able to stop the diagonal from the middie with the ball to
  2. He must remember he is a triangle to the ball and should
  not be flat on a low crease. D2 anticipates the pass being

made to the point man and reacts quickly to cover the ball in a harassing but controlled manner. It is important too that the defensive trailing middie stay out of the rotation and go to the hole area away from the ball, working inside out until adjustments are made.

Hold Call

There are times during the game when the defensive middie, D4, is close to 4 but not close enough to be all even. An alert defense will see this situation and make the audible hold call. The hold indicates to the defense that they do not rotate but instead lock into the attackman in their area. D6 plays a more centered position and anticipates the pass going to 6. At this time, he quickly and with control forces 6 with the ball. There is a strong indication that 4 will slow up with D4 catching up to him. The hold call can be made by an alert D6 or goalie. It may not get the ball back for the defending team, but it takes the offensive unit out of the fast-break scheme.

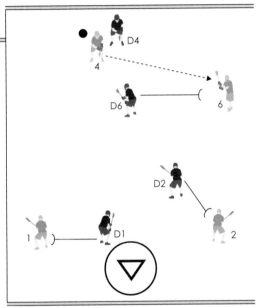

Figure 6.22 Hold Call

Riding

At one time, riding was a vital part of the practice schedule. This was because of the time element. There was an opportunity to make substitutions and to place defensive specialists in different riding packages. Having a clearing and riding segment of approximately forty-five minutes was highly common. With the change in the rules regarding putting the ball into play immediately after an out-of-bounds situation, it became somewhat difficult to get the specialists into the game. As a result, the strategy changed.

Although still an important phase of the game, riding has become more concentrated with limited time in the practice schedule. To eliminate any costly unsettled situations, as a result of offensive middies trying to substitute through the box, middies are required to stay in the contest when necessary and execute the appropriate ride. An important factor is to *keep things simple!* Applying too many variations might be detrimental to the progress of the team. A sound philosophy would be to have the following rides in the game plan:

- **Regular**—Basic ride. If no ride is called at the time of the clear, the regular would be the ride. The attack plays a three-across zone at the restraining line, the middies also play a three-across zone at the midfield, and the defense plays man-to-man with the attack.
- **Deep**—This ride can be used during a sideline clear, which is between the restraining line and the midfield line. The attack plays a three-across zone up at the midfield line, the middies play approximately five to seven yards deep across the midfield, and the close defense play man-to-man.
- **Variation**—Certain calls alert the riding positions to apply a different approach, either all together or one position at a time. An example of this would be the George call. The attack would play the two-wing attack down with the

George man upfield. In this scenario, wherever the ball is thrown, the George attackman doubles on the defender getting the ball.

- **Bump**—This is a full-field ride with the goalie coming out and covering the opposite attackman from the ball.

Regular Ride

This is a three-three ride involving the attack and the midfield. It is a flexible zone with the double coming after the first pass.

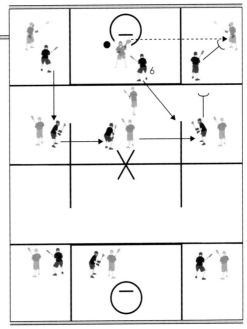

Figure 6.23 Regular Ride

- **Attack**—Plays in designated area. On the first pass to the defender, the onside attackman pressures the ball from the inside out, using the sideline. The offside attackman quickly drops back to the midfield line his side. 6, the middle attackman, runs a diagonal to the ball side.
- **Midfield**—The onside middie holds his position, reads the ride, and jumps down to double ball if needed. The middle middie quickly moves toward the onside alley to assist the onside middie. The offside middie quickly run to cover the vacated middle.
- **Defense**—The close defense rides man-to-man.

Variations

The close defense has three calls on rides: single, double, and regular.

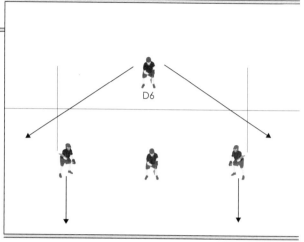

Figure 6.24 Variations

- **Single**—The crease defenseman comes up to the center midfield line. He is responsible to support 3 or 5 if they leave to double on the clearing defender. Both defenders play off their attackmen and watch the crease attackman. Goalie comes out to the restraining line. He could also take the weak-side attackman.
- **Bite-'em call**—Given by D6 or D1 and D2, this informs the onside middie that he can go up and double. D6, D1, and D2 support that area.
- **Double**—Both wing defenders, D1 and D2, move up toward the midfield line (approximately five yards before it, just outside the wing line). They are responsible for the middie in the alley and slide if 5 or 3 jump to double the clearing defender. The crease defender covers between his attackman and creaseman. The goalie picks up the weak-side attackman.

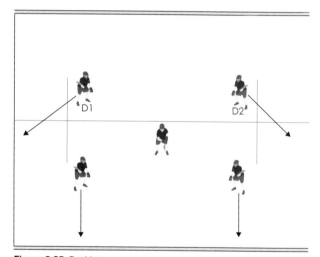

Figure 6.25 Double

- **Regular**—All three defenders play man-for-man with the attackmen.

Triangle (Double T)

RESPONSIBILITIES

- **6**—Picks up the goalie or ball. On the first pass, 6 releases quickly to double the ball.
- **1** and **2 (center backline)**—Split any center player above the crease. The onside attackman slides aggressively to the ball, trying to front the defender and receive support from the 6 attackman.
- **Offside attackman**—Slides hard toward the ball, picking up any player in the middle. On any cross-field pass to a defender, he becomes the force man.
- **1** and **2 (corner backline)**—The onside attackman picks up the ball, the offside attackman holds, and 6 replaces the onside attackman.

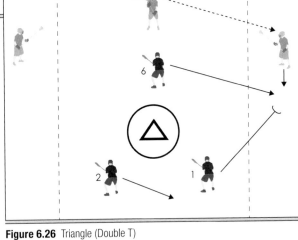

Figure 6.26 Triangle (Double T)

George

A nice change-of-pace type of ride. The attackmen play in a reverse triangle look, with the crease attackman playing five to seven yards above the restraining line (if the ball is behind the goal) and about five yards down from the midline (if the ball is in front of the goal). The George man (trap man) should be the best rider of the three attackmen. He should be instructed as to the proper way to pressure ride:

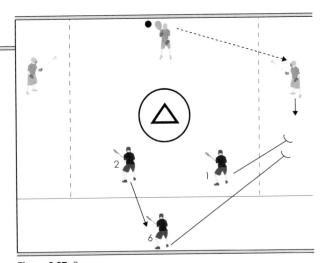

Figure 6.27 George

- Keep proper angle.
- Sprint hard to the ball carrier, but under control.
- Use the sideline as an extra player.
- Never give up the inside field.
- Do not overpursue.
- Anytime given the opportunity, run through the clearing person.
- Take away the defender's "good stuff."

Both wing attackmen play approximately five yards outside the crease, both sides, in a ball-behind situation and approximately twelve yards up from the goal in a front-of-the-goal setup.

Deep Ride

Quite often the deep ride causes havoc with the clearing team. It can also be used when teams are clearing at the midline or upper sideline. The attack is positioned at the midfield line in a sliding zone format. The midfield is stationed approximately five yards deep and pick up the first man over in their zone.

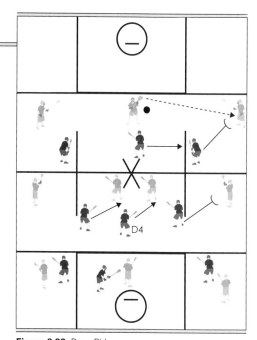

Figure 6.28 Deep Ride

RESPONSIBILITIES

- **Onside wing attack**—Supports his zone area and attack ball.
- **Offside wing attack**—Slides to replace D4's vacated middle area.
- **D4, middle middie**—Should be a long-stick if possible. Slides to the ball side, and picks up the near man or double ball.
- **Defense**—Plays man-for-man.

Midfield Options

- **Regular**—Basically a sliding zone format. All three midfielders play up on the midfield line, and each is responsible for his area. Once the first pass is thrown, the onside middie can slide to the ball or hold the man in his area. The middle middie slides to ball-side alley area to support. The offside middie contains vacated area left by middle middie. All three must be alert for calls from the defense.

    Example: The bite-'em call by wing D or diamond call (D6 informs 4, middle middie, that he can move ten yards toward the restraining line).
- **Red**—The red call is strictly a man-to-man call. There are certain times in the game when it is more appropriate to use the man-to-man call than the zone.

    A typical call might be the "single, red," which would give the D6 defender an option to double the ball coming over the midfield line
- **Double T**—Middies roll toward the first pass with the onside middie trapping the ball, while the middle middie and offside wing middie slide across the midline to vacant areas.

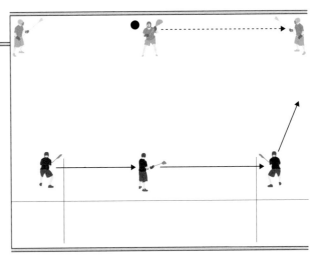

Figure 6.29 Midfield Options, Regular

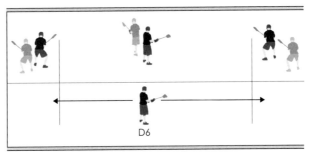

Figure 6.30 Red

Figure 6.31 Double T

Ten-Man Bump: Roll 1

The ten-man bump ride is highly aggressive and can be risky. Everyone must perform in a high-percentage manner. This ride has often been successfully executed by hiding it at the beginning, cutting off the best clearing defensemen, and leaving the weakest clearing defenseman open, as he is the most obvious player. The ideal situation is to get an aggressive long-stick, or the best defender, playing on this defenseman. The rider gives the defender enough cushion to draw the attention of the goalie for the pass. Once the pass is made, the long-stick attacks the ball. The attack cuts off obvious players, while the midfielders slide to the adjacent man to the strong side. The weakside defender, away from the first pass, bumps up and covers the farside middie in the alley. The onside defenseman and the crease lock on. The goalie should replace the weak-side defender and cover the attackman farthest from the ball. He should be alert of the ball movement and recover to the goal.

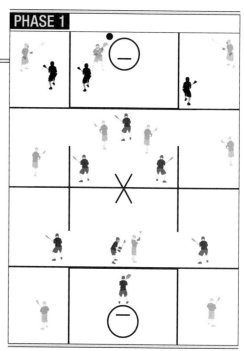

Figure 6.32 Ten-Man Bump: Roll 1, Phase 1

Figure 6.33 Ten-Man Bump: Roll 1, Phase 2

Ten-Man Bump: Roll 2

Another look, roll 2, can be very effective. The *onside riding* attack, middie, and defenseman bump up with the attack and the middie doubling the ball. The onside defender bumps up to cover the clearing middie in the onside alley. The far-side attackman sprints back to the midfield, taking away the cross-field pass. The far-side and middle middie cover the next-closest middie toward the ball. The close defense all rotate to the ball side with the onside defender bumping up. The stopper covers the far-side attackman.

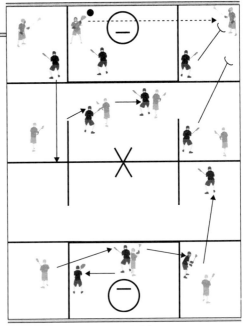

Figure 6.34 Ten-Man Bump: Roll 2

Transition of Defensive Midfield

Many times during the contest, with the ball in transition, the defensive midfield has brought the ball down to the offensive end, with the offensive midfield forced to play defense. In this scenario, it is advantageous to keep the offensive middies on the field as long as possible. Therefore, it is a definite advantage to substitute out by going to the midfield instead of the box area. It stands to reason that a sprint from the center of the restraining line to the midfield, twenty yards, is more convenient than running to the penalty box, which is approximately thirty-two yards. This type

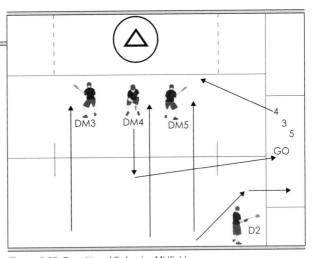

Figure 6.35 Transition of Defensive Midfield

of substituting enables the offensive team the advantage of working against a very inexperienced defensive group.

RESPONSIBILITIES (assuming all three defensive middies are on the offensive end)

- **D2 or closest defender to the penalty box**—Quickly stations himself right at the box corner, looking for the first substituting D-middie to cross the midfield. Simultaneously, he steps into the box area, giving a "go" call to the substituting middie, 4. As soon as the DM4 middie comes to the box and off the field, D2 steps back on the field and resumes his position at the box corner, ready to repeat the move until all defensive middies are off the field.
- **DM5**—Replaces DM4 until it is his turn to substitute from the middle of the field.
- **DM4**—On the "middies off" call, DM4 turns from the 4 position and sprints to the midfield, thus releasing 4 to enter the game. He then exits through the box.
- **DM3**—Supports the ball until it is his time to exit. He then duplicates DM4's move.

Note: because of the timing element, it is important to include the "transition of defensive middies" segment in the practice schedule daily.

The Goalie

7

I **HOPE EVERY COACH COULD HAVE THE OPPORTUNITY OF** having his own youngsters on his team. I have been very fortunate to have coached my sons, Keith, Carl, and Curt, in wrestling, and that was a special time. It was also special to have Keith as a member of my Towson lacrosse team. I cherish the memories of the practices, games, trips, and the rides home just talking and sharing thoughts together. Keith was a good athlete and played the position of goalie. He probably could have started for a large number of schools, but he chose Towson at a time when we had one of the best goalies in the game. I was glad he did. He was great to have on the team, and never once did he tarnish his loyalty to his teammates by bringing stories home. He was a true teammate! He would laugh so very hard at the dinner table, as both his mother and grandmother would run me through the mill wanting me to justify why he wasn't starting or playing more. There were times when I just wanted to drop him off at the house and keep going! Those were special years.

I remember sitting at the dinner table years later discussing personnel with my wife, Joan. I mentioned one of the players in particular, because his parents and Joan and I had grown up together. We were good friends. The youngster, an outstanding player in high school, was highly independent and prone to do his own thing. In contrast, at Towson we had our own philosophy about how things should be accomplished. Bottom line, do it our way or sit the bench! I told Joan I was concerned about our relationship with the parents. I said we might lose our friendship with the couple because of their love and loyalty to their son. I remember stating, "You know, blood runs thicker than water!" Having said that, Joan jumped up from the dinner table and exclaimed in a loud voice, "That's bull crap! I *slept* with my son's coach for *four years*, and *my* son didn't play!"

Goalie Play: The Last Line of Defense

One of the most neglected areas in the game of lacrosse is the goalie position. Most likely, this is because coaches do not feel comfortable teaching this position and are limited in the desired knowledge. The goalie usually is given very basic drills

to perform during the early practice period and is eventually forgotten throughout the remaining time. As coaches, we want to assume the goalie knows exactly what to do in certain scenarios. This is a lot easier for us. If, as we say, the goalie is the most important person on the defense and is described as a coach on the field, a more determined posture should be taken in preparing the goalie to have a strong field presence. Coaches should stress basic fundamentals when working with their stoppers. Attention to these fundamentals should not be pushed aside for "more important things at the time." The five areas of importance that should be valued in the development of the goalie are:

- Orientation
- Saves
- Communication
- Seventh defenseman
- Outlet passes

Orientation

The stopper must know where the ball is at all times. He must be in the proper position and be set for every shot or feed. Position orientation is extremely important in goalie play. He must always be aware of the space relationship between himself and the goal. This is accomplished by marking the front of the crease at different points, usually three: at the front top and at both the right and left fronts. He can also create position references by "playing the pipes," since they are constant (i.e., always there).

A majority of goalies use the semicircle, an imaginary arc approximately three to four feet at the front center to the pipes. As the ball moves on the outer perimeter, the goalie moves on the semi-arc, always keeping his chest in line with the ball. As the ball moves to the side and behind, the stopper

must be aware of the feed more than of the shot. When the ball comes to the plane from behind, the goalie locks to the pipe, respecting the shot but thinking of the feed. He should always be in touch with the pipes.

Saves

High, on Side

The coach should be clear and concise as to what he wants the stopper to do. The fundamentals involved should be simple and directed toward good sound habits. It would be advantageous to have the goalie come out every day, before the others, to work on his skills (fifteen minutes). He should be pushed hard and in a positive manner. "Warm him up, don't

burn him out!" Too often stoppers are warmed up by individuals trying to impress the crowd or goalie as to how hard they can shoot the ball or how tricky they can be on the inside. Avoid this! Emphasize to your players that they should stay with the plan. The goalie must be given constant feedback, either right or wrong, in a constructive manner as to how he is performing.

The most important part of stopping a shot is being in the proper position. Some coaches like the stick in the middle of the body, at chin height, and to the stick side. A preference used by many coaches is to keep the stick shoulder high in the "box" position. It is important to lead with the stick and follow with the body. Applying a strong element of concentration, the goalie should follow the movement of the ball with his body.

On the shot, the stopper leads with the stick, follows with the body, and tries to completely engulf the ball. Whether a straight shot or a bounce, it is important for the goalie to keep the stick in a perpendicular position, allowing ultimate stick surface.

Bounce Shot

The emphasis on the bounce shot is to eliminate going to the knees. Good shooting teams generally have a field day with stoppers who go to the knees when trying to make the save. Players should remember to attack the ball, keeping the stick in a vertical position, and completely engulf the shot.

The One-on-One

With a shooter in close, it must be stressed that the goalie keep the goalie stick parallel to the shooter's stick. The height of the goalie stick should be placed with the *top frame just below the top of the shooter's stick*. (The goalie should keep in mind that the ball does *not* travel from the pocket through the top of the stick, but from the pocket to the target.) The goalie's body position should be *in front of the shooter's stick*, as a second line of defense, taking away as many advantages as possible. He should try to dictate through his body and stick position where the shooter will shoot. Take away a part of the net, and let him think the other part is open. Remember, *"Stick on stick—body on ball!"*

Head, Hands, and Feet

The goalie should move his head, hands, and feet as one. If they are consistently correct, the rest will follow.

- **Head:** Emphasize that the goalie has his head on every shot or pass, regardless of where it is. The head draws the body with it and forces the goalie to see the ball into the stick. Also, on low shots, it is important for the goalie to have his head over the ball, allowing his body to smother it.
- **Hands:** The hands should hold the stick with authority with the top hand at a high "neck" position. The hands and stick should be kept out in front of the body, not extended but in a bent-elbow, reaction-type manner. This enables immediate stick movement to the ball. Stick movement should be into and through the shot.
- **Feet:** The feet should be set and balanced for every shot or feed. The goalie should move his feet aggressively into the shot. It should be stressed here that forward momentum be a priority. Since the correct foot movement is so crucial, the goalie should be forced to step with the ball-side foot first, getting into its path and moving through the ball.

Communication

The key to successful defense is communication, and the goalie is the center of it all. He must understand the importance of talk and realize the difference his voice makes on the field. Just as he knows how important the skills of stopping shots are, he should realize that his voice is a major characteristic of good goalie play.

Stress the following fundamentals with your goalies:

- The voice should be loud and clear. Whatever information the stopper is trying to convey must be given in a powerful manner. He has to attract the attention of his defense.
- The goalie should speak with authority and demand response from defenders.
- He should avoid speaking in a monotone. Too many goalies make this mistake, which is detrimental to the defense.
- He should be specific. Short sentences are best. He should speak in the simplest way possible.
- He should emphasize what he wants.
- He should be positive, getting the defense to play for him and not against him. The goalie should use his voice in a positive manner and communicate constructively.

BASIC COMMUNICATION

The goalie should do the following:

- Identify the position of the ball.
- Tell the covering defender what his position is (e.g., "Square up," "Hold," "Check sticks," "Angles").
- Back up. Who are the primary and secondary backers (e.g., "Who's hot?" "Choke," "Bite 'em")?
- Identify what's happening (e.g., "Watch the dodge!").
- Initiate slides (e.g., "Get ready to go," "Fire!").
- Use the "Check sticks" call on all feeds.
- Describe the situation (e.g., "Ball's center front," "Loose ball").
- Immediately give the "Break!" call when gaining possession.

The coach must be conscious at all times of how his goalie is playing and communicating. The stopper must be informed as to his position play and how he is talking. Can he be heard? Is he understood? This should all be done in a positive manner. Many goalies have the athletic ability to be good stoppers, but they may lack some of the fundamentals that are needed to be outstanding. It is the position of the coach to make sure the stopper is given every opportunity to play to the best of his ability. Remember, a chain is as strong as the weakest link. Don't expect him to improve on his own—that's your job!

Seventh Defenseman

Besides being in control of the defensive end of the field, the goalie is in *total command* of the crease area. It is his responsibility to anticipate any and all situations that could occur. He must be in the proper body-and-stick position to block feeds from behind and across the cage. He should read eyes and predetermine where the feed is going. On feeds or passes, he must turn his head quickly, follow the ball, and be prepared to set up to attack the shot. The goalie must understand that he is the "director of activities" around the crease area when the ball is loose. Unsettled situations and loose ball play around the crease are to be played aggressively. The stopper should be ready to check sticks, clamp the lacrosse ball hard, hip out, and control and scoop the ball.

Outlet Passes

As a coach, playing against a stopper who is highly effective with his outlet passes is a big worry. It can change the momentum of the game instantly. With this in mind, it is beneficial to work hard with your goalie in this area. He must first be aware of how powerful a weapon the outlet pass is and then be willing to incorporate the pass into his arsenal. At times, this comes very naturally with some goalies. In most cases though, coaches have to really work at it. Practice time should be spent releasing the ball to both wing areas, along with the twenty-, thirty-, and forty-yard passes. It would be in the best interest of the team to do this daily.

FOUR KEYS TO IMPROVING OUTLET PASSES

- After gaining control of the ball, the stopper must look upfield immediately, see the entire field, and search for the best pass.
- The goalie must be patient. He should use the four seconds, let the play develop, and make the best possible pass.
- The goalie should move his feet! He should not stand still with the ball but move to get in the best position to make the pass.

- The goalie must develop the right touch on the pass. The ball must be put on the money. It cannot be overthrown or underthrown. Because of the situation, with the players

being spread the field, there is little margin for error. The
goalie should scan the middies first, then look to the sides
for the defensemen, and finally, take the ball himself, using
the crease as an advantage.

Outlet Pass Drill 1

- Quick breakouts.
- The coach shoots to the goal, and
  the goalie makes the save and
  passes to the breaking middie A.
  After catching the ball, the middie
  returns it to the coach and then
  travels to the B line.
- After the next save, the goalie calls
  out for a release by the B middie,
  who will release after the goalie
  makes the save. After catching the
  ball, he alternates lines.

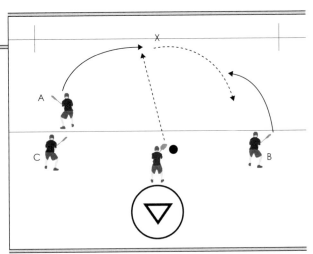

Figure 7.1 Outlet Pass Drill 1

Outlet Pass Drill 2

- This is similar to the preceding
  drill, except the players are in the
  center and alternately break out
  for the outlet pass.

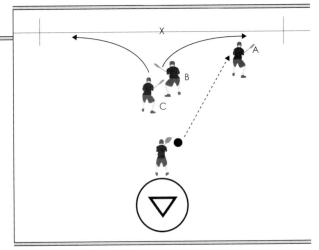

Figure 7.2 Outlet Pass Drill 2

Goalie Warm-Up Drills

Position: Three-Man—Front

Keep in mind these drills are position drills and should be executed after completing the shooting technique drills.

In the singles drill, with the ball in the front 4 position, the goalie should play a high arc or high-crease position, assuming the shot is going to take place. As the ball travels to the side of the crease, he quickly assumes an advantageous position on the pipe or in a one-on-one take-away stance. He works on his proper step procedure. The doubles drill is quite similar, with the stopper playing the feed to the 1 side of the crease. He then takes the proper steps and makes sure he executes the required movement on the second pass across the cage. He should first step with the upfield right foot, crossing over with the trailing left foot and closing the stance with the right foot.

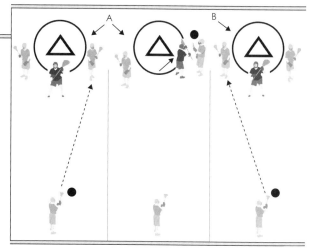

Figure 7.3 Three-Man—Front

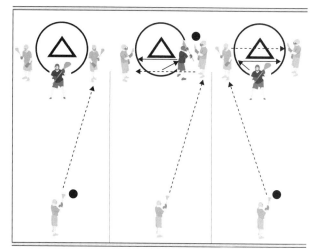

Figure 7.4 Three-Man—Front

Position: Three-Man—Behind

The goalie should keep his eye on the ball, communicate, rotate, and protect the pipes on the come-arounds. He must be aware of any feeds onside or offside and react accordingly. These are not fancy drills for the stopper. The purpose is to have him adjust in the proper manner with the ball in any position. The three-man selection for daily work with the stopper could be a defender, attack, and midfielder. However, the choice of the coach may be to keep the same crew with the goalie warm-ups at all times.

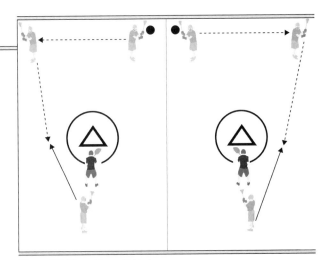

Figure 7.5 Three-Man—Behind

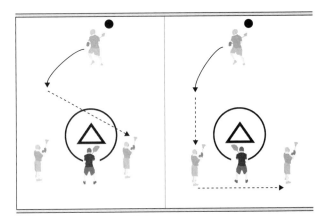

Figure 7.6 Three-Man—Behind

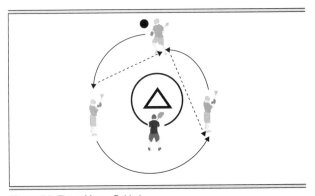

Figure 7.7 Three-Man—Behind

8

The Face-Off

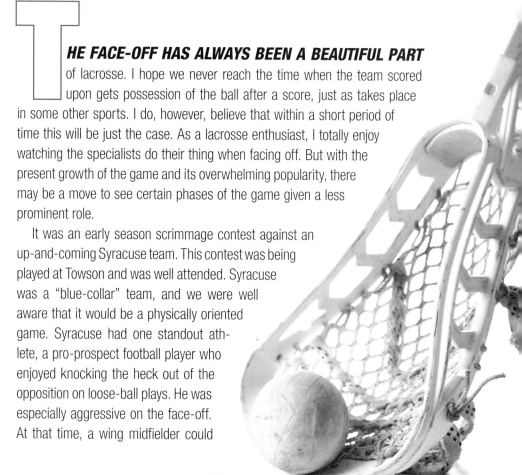

THE FACE-OFF HAS ALWAYS BEEN A BEAUTIFUL PART of lacrosse. I hope we never reach the time when the team scored upon gets possession of the ball after a score, just as takes place in some other sports. I do, however, believe that within a short period of time this will be just the case. As a lacrosse enthusiast, I totally enjoy watching the specialists do their thing when facing off. But with the present growth of the game and its overwhelming popularity, there may be a move to see certain phases of the game given a less prominent role.

It was an early season scrimmage contest against an up-and-coming Syracuse team. This contest was being played at Towson and was well attended. Syracuse was a "blue-collar" team, and we were well aware that it would be a physically oriented game. Syracuse had one standout athlete, a pro-prospect football player who enjoyed knocking the heck out of the opposition on loose-ball plays. He was especially aggressive on the face-off. At that time, a wing midfielder could play havoc on the opposing team's face-off man. This individual did just that. He would constantly inflict pain on our little draw man. It was to the point where I wanted to see him get stuck. We called a time-out, and in the huddle I informed the team of my strategy. "Get 'em back" time!

Joe Ferrante, a hard-nosed player who would run through a wall for you if you showed him which wall, was the designated assassin. I told Joe that on the face-off I wanted him to concentrate solely on the football player and not even worry about the ball. His mission was to knock the hell out of the big bugger! He was to sacrifice his body for the sake of the team. As they lined up for the face-off, the intensity was overwhelming. Our heat-seeking missile, Joe Ferrante, was ready to be launched. The whistle blew, and both teams converged to the middle. Then due to an infraction there was a second whistle to stop play. Everyone stopped and looked at the official . . . except Joe!

Zeroed in on his target, he just kept coming. The scene resembled something out of a race-car crash. The big football player got hit with a good shot and came up from the ground furious, trying to get at Joe. The official, Ron O'Leary, was more angry than the inflicted player. He grabbed Joe and shouted, "He's got a minute for unsportsmanlike conduct!" With my quick thinking, I shouted to O'Leary, "Ron, he didn't mean it. He's deaf!" Ronnie looked back and responded, "Yeah, he's deaf, but he's not dumb!"

Facing Off

The face-off is a deliberate technique used at the beginning of a contest, at the start of each quarter, and after each score. Its primary purpose is to award possession. Some enthusiasts have considered this phase of the game as the most exciting to witness. Since facing off is an integral part of the game and demands a unique skill, it is usually performed by specialists. These players are skilled at this type of exercise, and if highly efficient, they will

be strongly recruited. As previously stated, we at Towson University thrived on the percentage game, which is a game of ball control. Domination in the face-off area permits a team to maintain control and increase the shooting percentage. It is an opportunity to control momentum and execute the game plan. It can afford an average team the one tool needed to play respectfully against a more polished team.

The excitement of the face-off is usually evident in fourth-quarter play. Then this particular phase gives the team that is behind an opportunity to score, resulting in a closer score, a tie, or the lead. An opportunity that results from the controlled face-off is the fast break, or four-on-three situations. The combination of a controlled face-off and a fast break can eliminate leads and create a cushion in the score very quickly.

The luxury of having an outstanding face-off man is the result of practicing many hours with the proper technique. If a team is to be successful, one of the necessary properties is to have a good, fundamentally sound center midfielder.

Defensive Position at the Skirmish

Even though the face-off maneuver is completed by one player, the center middie, total execution involves the wing middies. They are an integral part of the completed action and must be conditioned to respond to the immediate situation. Though quite often the face-off specialist works individually and secluded from others during practice, the total picture involves the coordination and involvement of the wing middies. This is accomplished in a separate practice segment. Whether verbal or visual, communication by all three middies cannot be neglected here and is usually initiated by the center middie or the bench. If all three midfielders are in coordination with the call, the probability of success will increase.

The rules require that all the players facing off must have the left hand at the bottom position of the stick and the right hand at the top. The position of the wing midfielders is always the same. The wing middie to the right of his face-off man is referred to as the defensive middie. Many teams play a long-stick defenseman at this position. His main responsibility is to eliminate the fast break, be aggressive to the loose ball, be able to read the situation, and substitute on the fly when appropriate. The wing middie to the left of the face-off man is referred to as the offensive middie. His main objective is to be in a position to give support to the face-off middie. Mental alertness is a priority here as many ifs are involved. He must be prepared to react quickly to the offensive or defensive situation. Alert, aggressive wing personnel are vital to the success of lacrosse teams. Coordination of the face-off segment of the game, involving all three middies, should have priority in the practice schedule if high percentage is to be attained. A good face-off game plan eliminates confusion and increases individual and group confidence.

The Basic Face-Off Position

Though there are many different types of face-offs and counters, the basic position used in the draw should be consistent at all times and not vary. This position should meet each player's individual capacity for movement and not be for the benefit of the coach. Players should be given

the freedom to adjust and develop their own particular style. This is not to say the coach should restrict his input as to the execution of proper face-off technique, but the player should be exposed to the fundamental technique applied in the draw and at that time make any necessary physical adjustments.

Quick reaction to the whistle in an explosive manner, with the ball in control, is the desired result. The stance should be shoulder-width apart with the lead foot, the right foot, up close to the right hand, but not past it. The left foot can be closer to the right, if so desired. This enables the face-off man to step toward the head of the stick with the right foot at the sound of the whistle. This technique is also used as a defensive measure to hinder any movement toward the goal by the opponent. Comfort in the beginning stance is not important. The positions of the feet after the whistle has sounded and the quickness of the initial movement are the important elements to be sought. At this time, the stance should be balanced, with the hips low and the feet in a good athletic position and ready to react. At the beginning of the draw hips are turned slightly toward the head of the stick in an open look and should supplement quickness of movement in the initial reaction. Hand position varies according to the individual and technique to be used. Though some prefer the left hand approximately eighteen inches from the right, it is productive to position the left hand about six inches from the right. This distance allows more circular movement with the butt end of the stick and is vital in securing possession.

A good face-off man focuses on the task at hand. There can be no distractions. Concentration is of utmost importance if success is to be attained. The technique to be used should be predetermined against particular opponents, with any adjustments being made prior to the draw. Changing the grip while anticipating the whistle can be dangerous and result in loss of control. Therefore, face-off men are asked to concentrate on three things when approaching the draw position: remember the technique to be used, "read the wrist," and react to the whistle. Wrist reading can contribute keys as to what technique the opponent wishes to use. The wrist of the top hand, being on top of the stick at the twelve or one o'clock position and with the palm facing the opponent, indicates a rake move most of the time. In this case, the proper adjustment is made to counter such a move. If the position of the wrist is at three o'clock with the palm facing up, the tendency for the clamp is more prevalent and the appropriate counter should be used.

Face-Off Techniques

The Clamp

The most popular of all face-off techniques is the clamp. With all the changes in the face-off throughout the years, this technique has survived and is used very successfully. This move is not accomplished by the numbers—step-by-step—but is executed simultaneously. Weight should be distributed on both feet in close, with both hands lightly touching the ground. The right hand is over the ball with the palm facing up. The left hand should be close to the right hand with the palm facing down. On the whistle, the top hand rotates forward and clamps quickly, securing the ball to the ground, while at the same time the left hand punches forward, keeping low. The clamp should be with both hands. The initial push should come from the left foot, while the right foot steps forward and across the head of the stick. The face-off man should then be in a good breakdown position. An attempt should be made to push the ball between the legs; pivot on the right foot, placing the body between the ball and the opponent; and scoop through the ball.

Rake

The rake is a high-percentage face-off technique that demands time and practice. If time is put into mastering the move, it is well worth it. It is a quickness-type move. The basic stance in addressing the ball is identical to the clamp. All technique moves are simultaneous. On the whistle, the right hand, gripped up at the neck of the stick, is forced to the top end of the opponent's stick into the shooting string area. The right

hand should be pushed hard, digging in, as the left pulls hard, keeping in mind the left hand should be low. Using the push (right hand) and pull (left hand) quick movement, the ball should be released to the left side of the face-off man. At this time the right foot steps across and toward the ball, impeding the movement of the opponent.

Hop or Jam

Another quick move used as a change-up in the face-off is the hop. It basically comes from the same stance as indicated for the clamp, but without the overemphasis of the top handgrip. This move is executed with one objective: to get the crossover and get behind the opponent's stick as quickly as possible. At the sound of the whistle, the face-off man attempts to jam the top part of his opponent's stick, placing his cross between the ball and the opponent's stick. Once this is accomplished, he draws the ball back between his legs, pivots on the right foot to block out his opponent, and turns quickly to scoop up the ball.

Counter to the Power Clamp: Reverse Clamp

At times a face-off man may use the clamp all the time with no variations. This would be a good time to counter with the reverse clamp. Any success here may lead to a possible fast

break. The stance is the same as with the regular clamp, stepping with the right foot for defensive position. The top hand on the stick should be gripped near the neck with the palm facing the opponent. The bottom hand should be twelve or fifteen inches from the top hand with the palm facing the left foot. At the sound of the whistle, the right hand jams toward the ball with the bottom part of the wall and immediately turns up to a twelve-o'clock position. The right hand now pushes the ball down the line toward the side. In a simultaneous move, the bottom hand snaps, palm down, and immediately pulls the stick back. It is important at this time to step across with the right foot, hip out the opponent, and scoop the ball for control.

As has been stated previously stated, the three-man face-off group playing together is vital to the success of the team. Communication is of utmost importance here, and all three players should be on the same page. Communication can be accomplished by the specialist or the bench, and it can be either verbal or visual. Verbal communication is giving a live name call, like a vegetable or a fruit. Visual communication might be two hands together holding the stick in front of the body for the clamp or touching the helmet for the rake. The rate of success in winning control of the ball is higher when a team is able to communicate. The following three-man face-off drills are very easy to employ in the practice schedule and could help with ball control.

Offensive Strategy with a Dominant Face-Off

Cutoff (Bump)

Quite often, the draw man feels very confident about a certain technique and may tell his crew to cut off their immediate opponents. This gives him the opportunity to work his move, control the ball, and create a fast break. Both wing people line up close to the opponent and quickly try to jam, screen, or cut off that person.

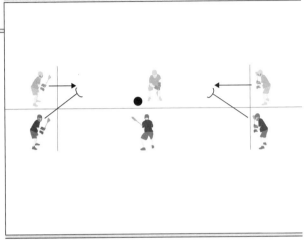

Figure 8.1 Cutoff (Bump)

Release

On the release, the face-off might be a draw ball with the draw man reverse pivoting, hipping out, and running to scoop the ball. As soon as he has control and an opportunity, he turns, looks upfield to the wings, and passes quickly. On the whistle, the wings drive in, read the situation, and turn upfield, looking for the pass.

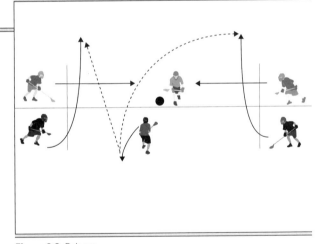

Figure 8.2 Release

Alley

The alley technique can be worked with a great deal of success and give the offense a two-on-one situation. The draw is executed between the legs and scooped up by the face-off man. He then turns and passes to the goalie, who promptly looks to get the ball to the 2 defender moving down the right alley. The alley should be an automatic anytime the face-off man is pressured and having trouble getting the ball upfield.

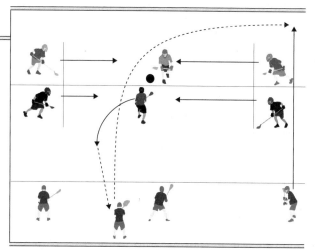

Figure 8.3 Alley

Catch 'Em

Quite often, the opposition get so caught up in the game that they lose concentration on the task at hand. This is a good time to exploit the situation with something like the catch-'em. The offensive middie sets back toward the sideline and at the last moment steps up on the line, running a diagonal on the whistle. The face-off man gains control and quickly passes to that middie. Surprisingly, this technique on a man-down face-off usually

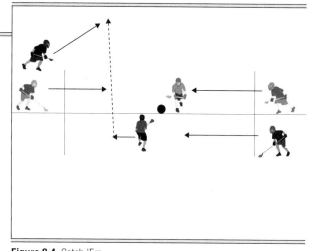

Figure 8.4 Catch 'Em

works well when having to bring the *attackman* up to the line. Calling out to that attackman, or middie, and telling him he is on the wrong side gives the impression that he doesn't know what he's doing and complements the play.

Defensive Strategy vs. the Dominant Face-Off Man

Cutoff

In using the cutoff, it is important to place the fastest defender at the cutoff position. All others play the natural position, trying to force the face-off man to his left before he drives downfield. It is vital that the defensive face-off man step hard to the right, cutting off the opponent and hoping to take away any immediate break.

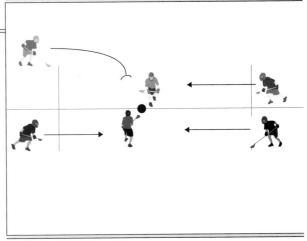

Figure 8.5 Cut Off

Rotate

The rotate is similar to the cutoff. The long-stick or short-stick middie plays to the end of the wing line, taking as much as he can. On the whistle, he sprints to the nearside restraining line, releasing the wing defender so the wing defender can switch to the crease man. The crease defender now is available to pick up the ball, controlling the face-off man. There can also be a rotation move where the long-stick middie plays the crease, the crease man plays the

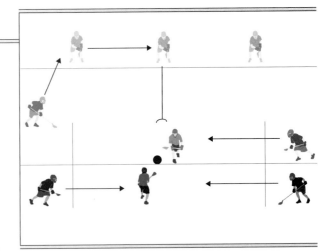

Figure 8.6 Rotate

2 position wing attackman, and the D2 defenseman moves to the wing. Here, all long-sticks end up with normal coverage.

Hey Joe

Hey Joe is an automatic double-team in normal play and also on the face-off. In the draw situation, everyone must be alert to their responsibilities. There can be no breakdowns. The two short-stick middies are responsible for the wing attackmen on their side. The two close defenders move up to the midfield. The defensive middie, D2, is responsible for locking onto the short-stick on his side. The long-stick is responsible for going after the face-off man. The face-off man (D4) steps laterally to the right to stymie any forward movement and jams the face-off man. He harasses vigorously, trying to work the movement back into the double-team. Attack 2 steps upfield and "zones covers" the long-stick with D3 on the other side.

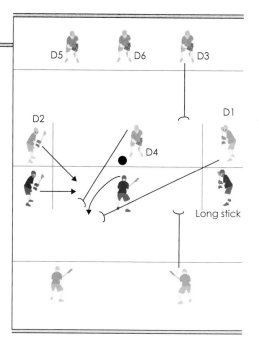

Figure 8.7 Hey Joe

These segment drills are fun to run, easy to teach, and productive in the game situations. They add another effective and efficient dimension to a team's ability to succeed.

9

Practice Organization

O**NE OF THE REWARDS OF COACHING IS SEEING** young people experience various circumstances of adversity and then grow in a positive manner from those situations. Coaches confidently anticipate a life-learning lesson, either good or bad, that might assist in the character development of these players. I recall one of those opportunities a few years back. My Towson team was playing a very good Johns Hopkins team at home in the evening. For our team to be successful, everything had to be right. That is, we had to play the percentage game: control the face-offs, slow the ball down, take high-percentage shots, avoid fouls, get the ground balls, and maintain a strong defense. Plus among other things, our stopper had to have the game of his life. It could be done!

Our game plan was simple. If we could stay close for three quarters, our momentum would carry us through the fourth. Also in our favor was the crowd. The stadium was packed, and they were looking forward to a great game. That's exactly what the kids gave them. Anytime we played Hopkins, our youngsters played hard.

Late in the fourth quarter, in a very close game, the momentum seemed to drift toward the Blue Jays. I was becoming frustrated with our kids, as were my assistant coaches, Joe Ardolino and Jeff Clarke. Both coaches came to me yelling, "Coach, we're losing it. We have to get the kids back on track! Call a time-out!" I was very upset at the turn of events and I totally agreed with both Joe and Jeff. I called for a time-out and started to walk out on the field. This was a super opportunity for the players to experience character development through coaching brutality.

As we walked to the center of the field, Joe started to bear to the right and called for all the offensive players to huddle around him. Jeff bore to the left and called for all the defenders. I stood in the middle of the field, like I had fallen out of a plane, with no one around me but a short, chunky, third-string goalie with his hand in a cast, waiting for me to give some kind of worldly advice about having pride, character, or something like that. I felt like I had every eye in the stadium on me at that point. It was a highly embarrassing moment. I looked down into the round, inquisitive blue eyes of the rotund goalie and said, "Son, if you walk away from me now, you'll never play lacrosse again in your life!"

I often wonder if that player gained any lifesaving experience at that time. I sure as hell did—that was the last time we went to offensive and defensive huddles!

Philosophy

During my interim period as lacrosse coach for Towson University, not much had changed regarding Towson's philosophy of the practice organization. Being involved with football coaching has helped in developing a pattern that gets the most out of the players and ensures maximum teaching and learning. It is important to be thorough when developing a practice plan that involves both the long-range plan and the daily plan.

Long-Range Plan

It is important for each coach within the program to know exactly what he wants to accomplish throughout the season. A criteria could be the following:

Strengths and weaknesses of personnel. Be aware of the strong and weak points of each individual player. Players should be placed in the proper positions that enable them to strive for maximum execution. Many times coaches ask players to do something they are completely unable to do. This kind of decision usually results in a breakdown in performance, lack of confidence, and above all, a negative experience. An example would be asking the right-handed outside midfielder to perform on the left front of the offensive formation, which means he would have to sweep with his left hand. This is a difficult maneuver to perform. In contrast, the same player approaching the goal from the other side of the formation might be more successful.

Offensive and defensive philosophy. The personnel could determine this in the following manner:

- Are you a run-and-gun, fast-break-style team?
- Does the defense dominate the field of play?

- Are you ball-control because of a weak offense or defense?
- Are your players inexperienced?

Consideration should be given to the goals for the season. The goals should be realistic. Unattainable goals never should be established. Such goals could be disappointing to the team, even though the season has been successful. The objectives should be short-term oriented. They are a means to an end. These stepping-stone objectives are important to accomplish the primary function. The long-term goals may be to end the season successfully in wins and culminate in a conference championship. Therefore, the short-term goals could be achieving weekly success.

Short-range goals. The following should be of highest priority:

- Develop a practice plan.
- Implement the practice plan.
- Include the following: individual fundamentals, position play, six-man offense, six-man defense, team-oriented segments, extra-man offense and defense, fast break, face-off play, riding and clearing, and special situations.

These important factors play special roles in the overall plan. If a program is to have success, it is imperative to have a basic plan from which to work.

Practice-Time Scale

Practice-time schedules vary from coach to coach, whether in college, high school, or the junior program. Some are prolonged for two and a half hours, while others can accomplish, or must accomplish, the workout in a short period of time—an hour or less, because of school scheduling issues. I have found success with the two-hour practice schedule, both at the college and high school levels. The ultimate goal is to cover all the phases of the game during the course of a practice. This, however, is quite difficult, so some areas are placed on the alternate-day schedule. The schedule should be flexible to meet the *immediate* needs of the team. Because of the attention span of most athletes, it is in the team's best interest to keep drills and segments short; this achieves maximum efficiency.

Table 9.1 *Practice Time*

Activity	Time per Day (in minutes)	Days	Weekly Amount (in minutes)
1. Fundamental period (warming up)	10	5	50
2. Tendency period (one-man position play)	10	5	50
3. Position play (three-man play)	10	5	50
4. Fast break (progression drills—slow break, etc.)	10	5	50
5. Team-oriented segments (full field/clearing and riding)	45	5	225
6. Six-man offense/six-man defense (worked simultaneously)	15	5	75
7. Extra-man offense/extra-man defense (worked simultaneously)	10	5	50
8. Special situations (two-minute drill, game tricks)	10	5	50

Master Plan

Offense

VS. MAN-TO-MAN
1. Attack
2. Midfield
3. Combination—attackmen and middies
4. Six-man

VS. ZONE
1. Attack
2. Midfield
3. Combination—attackmen and middies
4. Six-man

CLEARING
1. vs. six-on
2. vs. deep ride
3. vs. bump

SPECIAL SITUATIONS
1. Two-minute drill
2. Husky
3. Man-down clear: defensive end
4. Man-down clear: offensive end

Defense

MAN-TO-MAN
1. Slides
2. vs. various formations
3. Cutoffs
4. Combinations

ZONE
1. Basic
2. Change-up zones
3. Combination
4. Special situations

RIDING
1. Basic
2. Traps
3. Seven-man
4. Deep
5. Bump
6. Special situations

Extra-Man Offense

1. Regular time
2. Short time
3. Special situations

Extra-Man Defense

1. Regular
2. Four-man box
3. Special situation

Practice Schedules

The following are examples of daily practice schedules used at the beginning of the season. Also detailed are the drills involved in each of these practices:

Table 9.2 *Practice Schedule—First Day*

Attack	Midfield	Defense
ALL PLAYERS Flexibility		
ALL PLAYERS Run—short sprints (40 yards in 10-yard COD lengths, 4 times)		
ALL PLAYERS Two-man passing—stationary (20 yards, hard passing)		
ALL PLAYERS Two-man passing—running (two lines, 20 yards apart, goal to goal)		
ALL PLAYERS Three-man weave—running (two lines, 20 yards apart, goal to goal)		
Scooping/passing	Line drills	Scooping/passing
ALL PLAYERS Tendencies		
COD—powers—rolls	Sweeps, splits, COD	Strong side/weak side
Four-on-three box	Four-on-three box (stress defensive positioning)	Four-on-three box
ALL PLAYERS Water		
Clearing/riding—regular—regular deep—34 ride—regular		
One-on-one (defense) behind	One-on-one (midfield) up top	One-on-one (attack) behind
ALL PLAYERS Evaluate		
Two-thirds full field (use a 60-yard field)	Two-thirds full field (use a 60-yard field)	Two-thirds full field (use a 60-yard field)
ALL PLAYERS Evaluate		
ALL PLAYERS Run—10/80s		
ALL PLAYERS GO IN "Head for the barn!"		

Table 9.3 *Practice Schedule—Second Day*

Attack	Midfield	Defense
ALL PLAYERS Flexibility		
COD	Short sprints	COD
Scooping/passing	Three-man line drills	Scooping/passing
ALL PLAYERS Two-man passing—stationary		
ALL PLAYERS Two-man passing—running		
ALL PLAYERS Three-man weave—running		
ALL PLAYERS Tendencies		
COD—powers—rolls	Sweeps—splits—COD	Box and rifle technique, strong side/weak side
ALL PLAYERS Four-on-three box		
ALL PLAYERS Water		
Offense (skeletal)—cut the post down	Offense (skeletal)—cut the post down	Defense (skeletal)—man-for-man
ALL PLAYERS Loose-ball fast break		
ALL PLAYERS Two-on-three/three-on-four—half field		
ALL PLAYERS One-on-one—four corners		
ALL PLAYERS Evaluate		
ALL PLAYERS Two-thirds full field (use a 60-yard field)		
ALL PLAYERS Run		
ALL PLAYERS GO IN "Head for the barn!"		

Table 9.4 *Practice Schedule—Third Day*

Attack	Midfield	Defense
ALL PLAYERS Flexibility		
COD	Short sprints	COD
Scooping/passing	Three-man line drills	Scooping/passing
ALL PLAYERS Two-man passing—stationary		
ALL PLAYERS Three-man weave—running		
ALL PLAYERS Tendencies		
COD—powers—rolls	Sweeps—splits—COD	Box and rifle technique, strong side/weak side
ALL PLAYERS Four-on-three box		
ALL PLAYERS Water		
(skeletal) Cut the post down, introduce 30- and 70-series slides	(skeletal) Cut the post down, introduce 30- and 70-series slides	(skeletal) Man-for-man, stress backup
ALL PLAYERS Loose-ball fast break		
ALL PLAYERS Two-on-three/three-on-four—half field		
ALL PLAYERS Three-on-three		
ALL PLAYERS Evaluate		
ALL PLAYERS Two-thirds full field (60 yards)		
ALL PLAYERS Run		
ALL PLAYERS GO IN "Head for the barn!"		

Table 9.5 *Practice Schedule—Fourth Day*

	Attack	Midfield	Defense
10 minutes	**ALL PLAYERS** Flexibility		
7 minutes	COD	Short sprints	COD
7 minutes	Scooping/passing	Three-man line drills	Scooping/passing
	ALL PLAYERS Two-man passing—stationary		
5 minutes	**ALL PLAYERS** Tendencies		
	COD—powers—rolls	Sweeps—splits—COD	Box and rifle technique, strong side/weak side
15 minutes	**ALL PLAYERS** Two-on-three/three-on-four—half field		
15 minutes	Attack vs. defense	Midfield vs. midfield	Defense vs. attack
	ALL PLAYERS Evaluate		
10 minutes	**ALL PLAYERS** Clearing and riding		
	ALL PLAYERS Review		
	ALL PLAYERS Water		
15 minutes	Offense (skeletal)—review, intro 24	Offense (skeletal)—review, intro 24	Defense (skeletal)—man-for-man
10 minutes	**ALL PLAYERS** Clearing/riding		
20 minutes	**ALL PLAYERS** Half field		
	First attack/first midfield vs. second defense	Rotate offense at 15 minutes	First defense vs. second attack/second midfield
	ALL PLAYERS Run		
	ALL PLAYERS GO IN "Head for the barn!"		

Table 9.6 *Practice Schedule—Fifth Day*

	Attack	Midfield	Defense
10 minutes	**ALL PLAYERS** Flexibility		
7 minutes	COD	Short sprints	COD
15 minutes	Scooping/passing	Three-man line drills	Scooping/passing
	ALL PLAYERS Two-man passing—stationary		
5 minutes	**ALL PLAYERS** Tendencies		
	30 series, post-bump-scrape technique	70 series, 70-Jack, shorty-loop	Introduce banana and follow technique
15 minutes	Attack vs. defense	Midfield vs. midfield	Defense vs. attack
	ALL PLAYERS One-on-one		
	ALL PLAYERS Four corners		
	ALL PLAYERS Banana/follow		
15 minutes	**ALL PLAYERS** Two-on-three, three-on-four—half field		
10 minutes	**ALL PLAYERS** Loose-ball fast break		
	ALL PLAYERS Water		
15 minutes	Offense (skeletal)—navy, review intro 24-spike	Offense (skeletal)—navy, review intro 24-spike	Defense (skeletal)—man-for-man slides
10 minutes	**ALL PLAYERS** Clearing/riding		
	ALL PLAYERS Cover regular/33 post Mike/43/sideline clears		
	ALL PLAYERS Half field		
	First attack/first midfield vs. second defense	Rotate offense at 15 minutes	First defense vs. second attack/second midfield
20 minutes	**ALL PLAYERS** Full field		
	ALL PLAYERS Run		
	ALL PLAYERS GO IN "Head for the barn!"		

Table 9.7 *Practice Schedule—Sixth Day*

	Attack	Midfield	Defense
10 minutes	**ALL PLAYERS** Flexibility		
7 minutes	COD	Short sprints	COD
15 minutes	Scooping/passing	Three-man line drills	Scooping/passing
	ALL PLAYERS Two-man passing—stationary		
5 minutes	**ALL PLAYERS** Tendencies		
	30 series, rifle-post-bump-scrape	70 series, 70-Jack, shorty-loop	Box technique, strong side/weak side
15 minutes	**ALL PLAYERS** Clearing drill		
	ALL PLAYERS Full team/full field		
	ALL PLAYERS Cover behind goal clears		
	ALL PLAYERS Restraining line		
	ALL PLAYERS Sideline		
15 minutes	Offense skeletal review: cut/post/down 24 and spike	Offense skeletal review: cut/post/down 24 and spike	Defensive reaction vs. 2-2-2 and 1-4-1, emphasize quick slides and talk
	Attack vs. defense	Midfield vs. midfield	Defense vs. attack
	1 on 1-3-3	Midfield face-offs	1 on 1-3-3
	Use diagrams	Positioning	Use diagrams
20 minutes	**ALL PLAYERS** STX substitutions		
	ALL PLAYERS On a clear		
	ALL PLAYERS Face-off substitutions		
	ALL PLAYERS Water		
10 minutes	**ALL PLAYERS** Half-field defensive reaction vs. 1-4-1		
	ALL PLAYERS Full field		
	ALL PLAYERS Run		
	ALL PLAYERS GO IN "Head for the barn!"		

Table 9.8 *Practice Schedule—Seventh Day*

	Attack	Midfield	Defense
10 minutes	**ALL PLAYERS** Flexibility		
7 minutes	COD	Short sprints	COD
15 minutes	Scooping/passing	Three-man line drills	Scooping/passing
	ALL PLAYERS Two-man passing—stationary		
5 minutes	**ALL PLAYERS** Tendencies		
	30 series, rifle-post-bump-scrape	70 series, 70-Jack, shorty-loop	Box technique, strong side/weak side
	ALL PLAYERS Clearing drill		
	ALL PLAYERS Full team/full field		
	ALL PLAYERS Cover behind goal clears		
	ALL PLAYERS Restraining line		
	ALL PLAYERS Sideline		
15 minutes	Offensive skeletal review	Offensive skeletal review	Defensive reaction versus 2-2-2 and 1-4-1
	Add 40 stack, 24 post, diamond	Add 40 stack, 24 post, diamond	Emphasize quick slides and talk
	Attack vs. defense	Midfield vs. midfield	Defense vs. attack
	1 on 1-3-3	Midfield face-offs	1 on 1-3-3
	Use diagrams	Positioning	Use diagrams
20 minutes	**ALL PLAYERS** STX-substitutions		
	ALL PLAYERS On a clear		
	ALL PLAYERS Face-off substitutions		
	ALL PLAYERS Water		
10 minutes	**ALL PLAYERS** Half-field defensive reaction vs. 1-4-1		
	ALL PLAYERS Full field		
	ALL PLAYERS Run		
	ALL PLAYERS GO IN "Head for the barn!"		

Table 9.9 *Practice Schedule—Eighth Day*

	Attack	Midfield	Defense
10 minutes	**ALL PLAYERS** Flexibility		
7 minutes	Scooping/passing	Three-man line drills	Scooping/passing
	ALL PLAYERS Tendencies		
	30 series, rifle-post-bump	70 series, 70-Jack, shorty-loop	Box technique, strong side/weak side, banana/follow
15 minutes	**ALL PLAYERS** Clearing drill		
	ALL PLAYERS Full team/full field		
	ALL PLAYERS Cover behind goal clears		
	ALL PLAYERS Restraining line		
	ALL PLAYERS Sideline		
15 minutes	Offensive skeletal review	Offensive skeletal review	Defensive reaction vs. 2-2-2 and 1-4-1
	Add 40 stack, open 24, corners	Add 40 stack, open 24, corners	Emphasize quick slides and talk
15 minutes	**ALL PLAYERS** Clearing and riding		
	ALL PLAYERS Full-field riding (George), single—double		
	ALL PLAYERS Water		
15 minutes	**ALL PLAYERS** Hey Joe explanation/demonstration		
10 minutes	**ALL PLAYERS** Half-field defensive reaction vs. 1-4-1		
15 minutes	EMO		EMD
	Cover 3-3, tight coverage		Cover 3-3
	Load/carry, 33 Jack		1-4-1
15 minutes	**ALL PLAYERS** Full field		
	ALL PLAYERS EMO vs. EMD		
	ALL PLAYERS Sprints		
	ALL PLAYERS GO IN "Head for the barn!"		

Practice Drills

Tendencies

Each position has "move" tendencies. It is our philosophy at Towson that the most popular moves should be practiced daily to make these moves automatic and improve reaction to various situations. The following position tendencies may be useful.

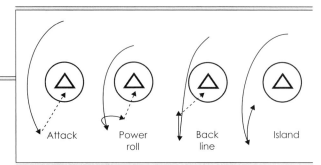

Figure 9.1 Position Tendencies

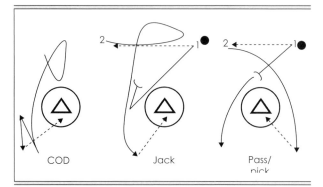

Figure 9.2 Position Tendencies

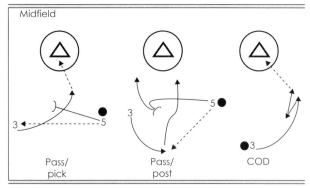

Figure 9.3 Position Tendencies

Defense

Banana Technique

The banana technique is a sound defensive move that teaches defenders not to give up the inside and to increase defensive pressure by switching hands to take away the onside shot. An example would be the defenseman playing the ball carrier at the wing position (see Figure 9.5) with the stick in his right hand. As the offensive player starts toward the goal on a banana cut, the defender keeps the inside position, switches hands, and rifle-checks, taking away any move by the attacker to switch hands and take the shot.

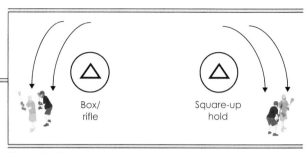

Figure 9.4 Defense

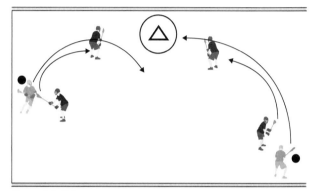

Figure 9.5 Defense

Follow Technique

Any time a defender is beat or behind his opponent, the defender will use the follow technique. The chasing defender places his cross directly above the helmet of the attacker. He waits for stick exposure and will diagonally check the stick.

Figure 9.6 Follow Technique

Four-on-Three Drill

This is an excellent opportunity to teach the fundamentals of defensive rotation and a good forerunner to progression drills (e.g., five-on-four, six-on-five). Start with the three-man rotation. On the four-on-three, the three defensemen always form a triangle facing the ball. They must never turn their back to the ball. Do not let the offensive players skip a pass, as this confuses the defensemen. Make sure the players are always talking: "I have the ball." "I have you backed to your right." "I have you backed to your left."

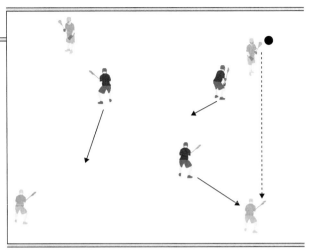

Figure 9.7 Four-on-Three Drill

Five-on-Four Drill

With the ball out front, the two wing close defenders are responsible for the crease attackman. When the ball reaches the attack, the middies are responsible for the crease. In this case, it would be a 1-3 defensive formation to the ball.

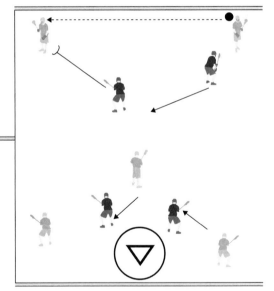

Figure 9.8 Five-on-Four Drill

Three-on-Two—Alternate Sides

This is a super three-on-two progression drill that helps both the offense and the defense. Offensively, it teaches patience and only the uncovered man is allowed to shoot. Defensively, it forces the defenders to support each other and to be in the right position to cover whoever gets the ball next. After one side finishes by scoring or by a defensive stop, the other side starts immediately. After a few rotations, the next players in line get into play. After this drill has been running for some time, the intensity picks up when an extra man is added both on offense and on defense and going four-on-three.

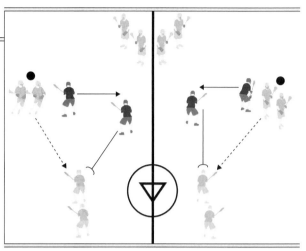

Figure 9.9 Three-on-Two—Alternate Sides

Four-on-Three—Alternate Sides

In this four-on-three drill, the defenders are asked to cover a different formation. The players on the left, offensively, are 1, 2, 3, and 5. They move the ball around until they are open to get the shot.

Defensively, there must always be a triangle to the ball and it is important to *talk*! Once this side has completed, the other side is quick to start. The two middies, 3 and 5, are always in the game for both the right and left sides.

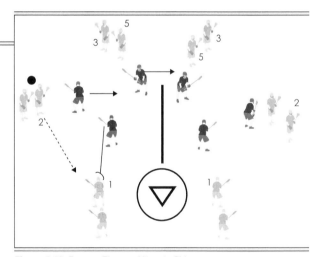

Figure 9.10 Four-on-Three—Alternate Sides

249

Slow Break—Green Drill

This excellent half-field drill conditions players to be in the right position at the proper time. The drill should end up with the offense in a 1-4-1 formation.

RESPONSIBILITIES

- **4**—Starts with the ball at the midfield. Once he is picked up by a defender, he passes the ball to either side. After the pass, 4 continues to read the situation and cuts to the open side of the crease, looking for a feed from point behind.
- **3**—Assuming he receives the ball from 4, he passes to the onside wing attackman and rotates to the 4 position in the middle.
- **5, offside middie**—With the ball away from him, 5 continues down to the wing position and expects a pass from point behind. If he doesn't have the shot, he transfers the ball to the 4 position.
- **6**—Cuts to the opposite side of the crease away from 4.
- **1**—When 1 receives the ball, he quickly transfers the ball to the point.
- **2**—He must cover the point behind when the ball is away from him.

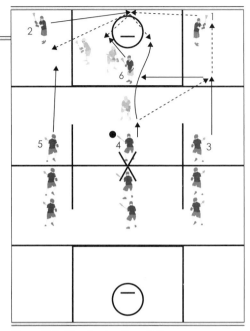

Figure 9.11 Slow Break—Green Drill

Note: this drill also can be run out of a 2-2-2 formation with the diagonal middies, 3 and 5, cutting to the ball behind.

Three-Man Line Drills

Three-man line drills are excellent for practice or game warm-ups. They include the whole team, with each drill eventually executed individually by each player.

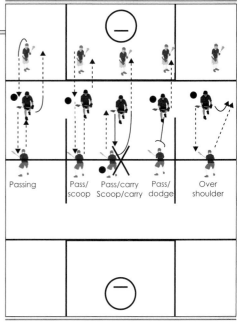

Figure 9.12 Three-Man Line Drill

Three-on-Two: Full Field

This is a great conditioning and stickwork drill that involves the full team with all players participating. To set up, goals are set approximately fifty to sixty yards apart. Players 3, 4, and 5 bring the ball down. D1 and D2 are on defense. Whoever takes the shot returns to the end of the line, his side. The remaining two offensive players switch over and play defense, sprinting to the far goal to set up.

On the shot, the two defenders (D1 and D2) rotate out and three new players (3, 4, and 5) come in quickly to play offense. Play continues at the other end.

This drill is also excellent for evaluating players and improving game reactions.

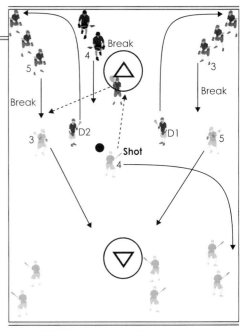

Figure 9.13 Three-on-Two: Full Field

Fast-Break Offense

Two lines of middies are aligned at or between the far-side midfield line and restraining line. The fast-break middie is across the field. Whoever comes up with the ball passes quickly to the far middie to start the break. Another group can be set up on the opposite side going in the opposite direction.

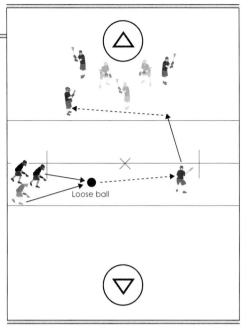

Figure 9.14 Fast-Break Offense

Full-Field Clearing Drill

This is a team drill with all players substituting in after each group clears the ball. Middies enter from the midline, defensemen enter from the clearing end, and attackmen enter from the scoring end. This drill becomes a starting drill at practice. Running, stickwork, and position technique are accomplished here. All clears are run in a sequence starting from behind the goal to in front of the goal, and finally at the midline. Quick passes are stressed, and each clear from behind and in front is timed (eight to twelve seconds from behind; eight seconds from in front of the goal).

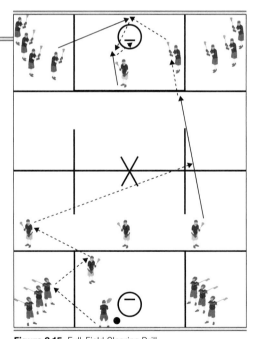

Figure 9.15 Full-Field Clearing Drill

Four Corners: Banana-Cut Technique (Offense and Defense)

Offensive players are asked to force the banana-cut move. They are expected to run the curl, protect their stick, and anticipate any move by the defenseman that will give them an opportunity to get an inside position.

The defenseman is expected to maintain an inside position. If his opponent has the stick in the hand of the opposite side, the defender is expected to switch hands. By doing this, the defender can penetrate deeper with his check. It also teaches the defenseman not to get caught going overhead or behind.

Substituting players should be behind their lines and ready to go. Lines alternate.

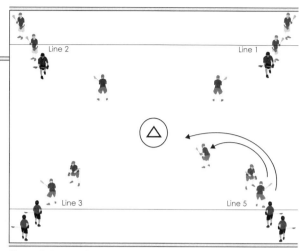

Figure 9.16 Four Corners: Banana-Cut Technique (Offense and Defense)

Face-Off Drill

This drill teaches wing players how to align after the face-off.

RESPONSIBILITIES

- **Offensive middie**—Always to the left of the face-off middie
- **Defensive middie**—Always to the right of the face-off middie

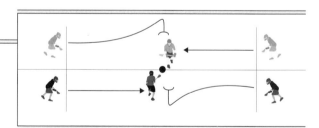

Figure 9.17 Face-Off Drill

Hey Joe Call

On a Hey Joe call, the offensive mid-die doubles the ball. The long-stick locks on. If this is a predetermined call, the long-stick middie switches positions with the short-stick. The 2 attackman and the 1 defenseman come toward the midfield to defend any pass by the face-off man to his defensive middie. All others lock on.

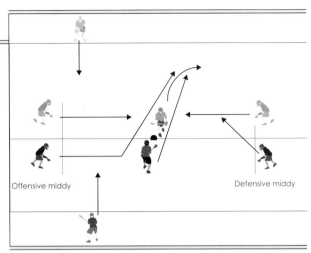

Figure 9.18 Hey Joe Call

Hey Joe Drill

The hey Joe drill is a quick-hitting "alley trap" executed when the offensive middies are bringing the ball over the midline and to the offensive end. It can be coached as an auto-matic jump or be a predetermined call by D4.

RESPONSIBILITIES

- **Onside close and crease defenseman**—Cut their man off from the ball.
- **Far-side close defender**—Split the distance between the attackman on his side and the upfield open middie.
- **D4**—Makes the call and starts to prerotate to the ball. Once 3 is in the alley area, D4 commits to trap.
- **D3**—Prerotates and cuts off D4's man, 4.
- **D5**—Pressures ball, and forces 3 to turn back upfield.

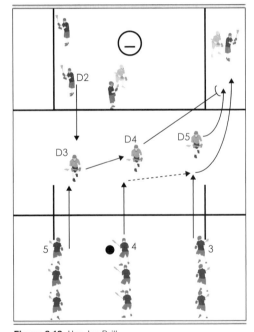

Figure 9.19 Hey Joe Drill

Shooting Drills

Quick Crease Shooting Drill

The player doing the shooting begins in the offside crease away from the feed. He must be ready to catch and shoot with accuracy. After every attempt, he must turn to receive a quick feed from the other line. When both lines have completed the feeds, a new player takes over in the crease. Placing a goalie in the cage increases intensity and accuracy. Feeders are approximately twelve yards from the crease.

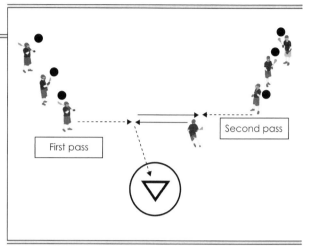

Figure 9.20 Quick Crease Shooting Drill

Split-Dodge Shooting Drill

The offensive player drives hard right and diagonally; on fronting the defensive player, he plants the right foot, changing directions in a diagonal manner. At the same time as the change of direction (COD), the stick is shifted from the right side to the left. It is important to protect the stick at this time.

The same technique is applied when the offensive player approaches the second defender, but reversed. After completing both split dodges, the offensive player prepares to finish with a positioned shot.

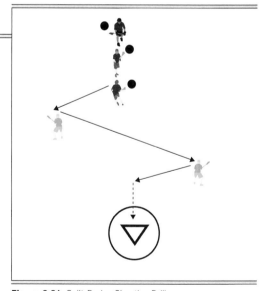

Figure 9.21 Split-Dodge Shooting Drill

Come-Arounds

- **Power come-around (CAR)**—Player must be aware of position and should be upfield approximately four yards past the plane. The shooter must have his outside foot upfield for maximum body torque and power. Stick position should be at twelve o'clock, one o'clock, or two o'clock.

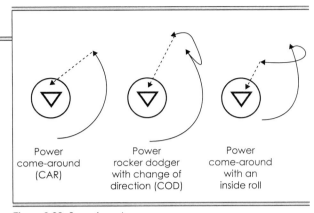

Power come-around (CAR)

Power rocker dodger with change of direction (COD)

Power come-around with an inside roll

Figure 9.22 Come-Arounds

- **Power rocker dodger with COD**—Once the carrier has broken the plane by four yards, he plants the inside foot, changes direction by taking one step with his outside foot, and then quickly changes direction again by pushing off the outside foot. Then he should step inside, toward the center with the inside foot, turn, and shoot.

- **Power come-around with an inside roll**—Once the carrier has broken the plane by four yards, he plants the inside foot and takes a depth step toward the goal with the outside foot. During this move, he continues to hold the stick with the outside hand. Once he has cleared the defender, he can place the stick in the appropriate hand. As he approaches the goal, he should determine his shot selection.

Figure-Eight Scoop-and-Shoot

The shooter starts approximately eighteen yards out in front of the cage. The balls (four) are placed at twelve yards in front and fifteen yards apart. The shooter starts to the left and scoops up the first ball, and rolls back upfield and across the middle, ready to fire a shot. After the shot, while on the move he then continues to drive to the next ball, scooping, turning upfield, and sweeping across for the second shot. This is continuous for four shots.

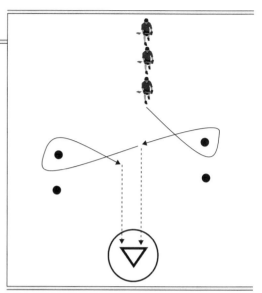

Figure 9.23 Figure-Eight Scoop-and-Shoot

Long Shots

High-Percentage Bounce Shots

- **Feeder**—Feeds to shooter; then rotates to shooter's line. Does not interfere with the shooter.
- **Shooter**—Uses the given technique, and spot shoots, three to four yards out in front of the crease. Tries to place the ball just below the top pipe. Rotates to the feeder's line.

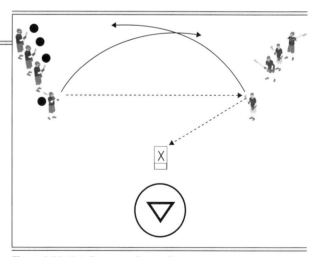

Figure 9.24 High-Percentage Bounce Shots

Long-Shots Shooting Drill

- **Feeding line**—Feeds to shooter, and then rotates to the shooting line. Does not interfere with the next feeder.
- **Shooting line**—Receives the ball, and uses proper technique in shooting. Rotates to the feeding line. Does not get in the way of the next feeder or shooter.

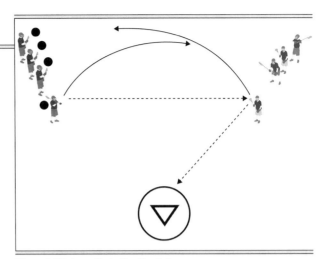

Figure 9.25 Long-Shots Shooting Drill

Crease Cutter's Drill

The cutter starts up top, one foot away from a cone placed ten to twelve yards above the crease. He cuts hard to the feeding position with an attackman on each side of the crease. He then receives a quick feed, shoots, and repeats the move, sprinting up around the cone and down again toward the feeder on the opposite side. This drill is repeated four to six times. This is an excellent drill for both the shooter and the stopper.

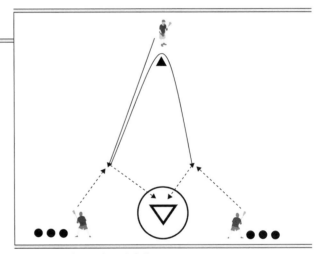

Figure 9.26 Crease Cutter's Drill

Three-Man Feed-and-Shoot

The Three-Man Feed-and-Shoot Drill is a progressive ball-movement drill broken down into three phases, as shown in Figures 3.27 and 3.28. Alternating feeds would have have the same drills being run on both sides.

1. **Feed attack**
2. **Feed middie**
3. **Feed crease**
4. **Alternate feeds**—work both sides.

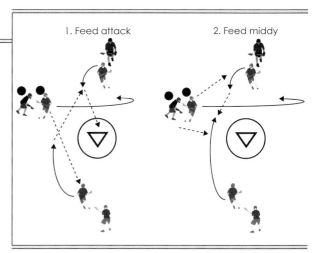

Figure 9.27 Three-Man Feed-and-Shoot Drill, Phases 1 and 2

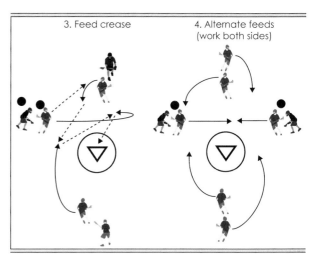

Figure 9.28 Three-Man Feed-and-Shoot Drill, Phase 3 and Alternate

Epilogue

I have been asked numerous times what have been my proudest moments in this great game. Though I have been fortunate to have a few, one seems to always take a front and center position. During his playing days, Danny Nolan was a big, dominant midfielder who gave us outstanding support and our players tremendous confidence in our style of play. He was a solid competitor, and I was glad he was with us. After graduation Danny assisted at Towson in a coaching capacity for about one year. He was named head lacrosse coach at the Christ Church School in Christ Church, Virginia, and later was appointed athletic director at the same school. At that time Danny was diagnosed with Lou Gehrig's disease. Though he fought the disease with every competitive fiber in his body, his physical condition became progressively worse. Danny succumbed to this tragic disease on March 9, 1992. I don't ever think of Danny without experiencing an overwhelming feeling of warmth, comfort, and peace of mind.

During the '91 quarterfinals in Charlottesville, Virginia, with Towson, ranked eleventh or twelfth, about to play the University of Virginia, I met Danny just outside the locker rooms. With Danny in his newly acquired wheelchair, we could cross the field and let him view the game from the sidelines. We won the contest, and I recall Danny telling me he couldn't make the next games but would surely be at the finals. I told him if we made the finals, he would be on the sidelines with us again. With an inspired bunch of young men, we made it to the finals!

The NCAA administrative meeting to cover the protocol of the event is usually held the day before the championship game. Present at this meeting were the administrative members representing both schools, the coaches, and the NCAA representatives. All areas of this spectacular were covered, and at the end of the meetings the NCAA representatives asked if we, the coaches, had anything to add. I said I had a concern. It involved bringing one of our people who was in a wheelchair onto the field, specifically to our sidelines. I was quickly informed that this could not be accomplished and that there was an area for wheelchairs only in the dome. For some unknown reason, I recall looking the administrator straight in the eye and exclaiming, "Then I hope you are totally aware that you are in violation of Public Law 94-142, the public law protecting the disabled!" (I was teaching sign language at the time and had just finished a lecture on this topic.) There was a pause of silence for a few seconds; then one administrator looked to a coadministrator and said, "You know, I don't see any problem with having this person on the sidelines, do you?" It was agreed Danny could view the games from our sidelines as long as he was out of the way of the players on the field.

As our players took the field for pregame warm-ups, I went to the players' entrance of the dome. Danny was there waiting for the large double-gate door to open. As the gate opened, we both entered the dome, moving diagonally across the field to our sidelines. I don't think I have ever been any prouder than at that moment—pleasant memories of an old friend.

Glossary

Adjacent man—The player to the right or left of the ball.

Alley—A term used for the area between the face-off wing line and the sideline. Also used to employ an across-field pass.

Angle—The defender overplaying the offensive player to the strong side, taking away the strength of the offensive player.

Axis of rotation—The ability to continue movement through a physical joint, as in the hips, shoulders, arms, and wrist.

Backer—This defender supports the hot man. Probably the most important man on the defense.

Banana—A defensive box technique that involves keeping the stick end always to the middle of the field. It is used to try to prevent the overhead check or go behind.

Bite 'em—A call from the hot man in pursuit to double the ball.

Black—A defensive call alerting the defense to play a particular zone. Black is a six-man zone defense.

Box—A position above the shoulder, stick side, approximately twelve inches high and twelve inches to the side.

Box technique—A technique used in close coverage that entails a number of designated moves used against the offensive player.

Bump—A move made by a defender moving from one player to another.

Carry—A term referring to moving the ball by the offensive player from one position to another with the expectations that the defender will follow.

Change-of-direction (COD)— An effective dodge within the restraining area. The technique involves a double change of direction to lure the defender out of position.

Choke—A defensive move by a wing defenseman coming across the crease to double, match up, or bite the come-around offensive player.

Clamp—A method of controlling a face-off by clamping the head of the stick over the ball.

Come-around—Power sweep from behind the cage. It is also referred to as the CAR move.

Cover—A defensive term referring to the man on the ball.

Cradling—A circular turn of the stick, usually toward the body, made by rolling the shoulder inward and rotating the wrist in a circular movement in the same direction.

Diamond—A formation on the fast break used occasionally when the fast-break middie is coming down the middle of the field. Also an offensive call for a six-man offense, as well as a defensive formation used in certain coverages.

Dizzy—A term informing the offense or defense that the defense is playing a zone.

Dodging—Certain offensive moves used to elude the defender.

Double—Informs the defense that the two wing defenders will move up on the ride. Two players versus one.

Double crease—Two players on the crease playing side-by-side.

Double-triple—An offensive formation placing three players on one side of the crease and midfield, with the other three on the other side.

Early—A fast-break middie having a cushion of about five yards or more. Once the pass is made to the point man, the close defense rotates. "Early" tells the point man to return the pass to the middie.

EMO—An extra-man offense usually encouraged by a penalty by the opposition.

Face dodge—A highly effective dodge in a crowd, with the stick being brought across the body in a strong cradling motion.

Face-off—A technique used to start the game after a score, or at the start of the first and third quarter.

Fast break—A transition opportunity with the team in control temporally having an extra man.

Fill—Usually the offside defensive midfielder. The third man of the defensive triangle.

Flat break—Highly proficient formation used occasionally on the fast break.

Follow-through—The flow of the bodily movement after the release of the ball.

Follow-defense—A beaten defender placing his cross over the top of the offensive player's helmet and chopping to one side or the other, depending on where the stick is.

Follow-EMO—Passing the ball and following the pass. Used a great deal on EMO.

Formations offense—Specific offensive sets that cause defensive turmoil.

George—Used primarily as a double screen. Also used as a trap on rides.

Gold—A five-and-one defensive zone.

Gringo—A specific clear from the offensive side of the midfield line when being double-teamed. Designated midfield clear.

Hey Joe—An automatic double team and slide used on the face-off, clearing, and regular play.

High-low post—Two offensive players on the crease, one low post, and the other playing a high post.

Hold—A fast-break call telling the defense not to rotate but to lock into their man.

Hop/jam—On the face-off, getting the crosse over and behind the opponent's stick as quickly as possible, and then drawing back.

Hot—The player responsible for sliding, backing, or doubling the ball. Sometimes known as the near man.

Husky—An undetected player coming into the game late from the box area while the game is going on—the husky man.

Iso—A term used by the offensive or defensive team regarding a one-on-one situation.

Iso-black—A defensive term used when there is a mismatch or isolation in front of or behind the goal. The defense then goes to an automatic coverage.

Jack—A specific call alerting the involvement of a screen or pick.

Leverage—The mechanics involved in shooting a lacrosse ball are of a first-class lever and include the position of the hands on the stick.

Lift check—Placing the defensive crosse under the opponent's bottom hand and lifting his stick.

Live color call—Can be used on defense or offense. Usually a call alerting the defense that if the players' paths cross, the defense will double the ball.

Lock on—Cutting off the adjacent players to the double team. Eliminating players from supporting the ball.

Match up—A call from the hot man to the cover man to release and go to the crease, picking up the first.

Match-up zone—A zone using the adjacent slides or rotation.

Mike—Another alert term specifically given to the middies. Can be used in all phases of the game.

Mike clear—A clear placing the middies at a specific position.

Moment arm—The distance from the top hand on the stick to the top of the stick head. Determines velocity.

Motion offense—A particular pattern where every player is involved with the offense in a moving manner.

Number series—An offensive scheme starting from 10 through 90, with each series having a different scheme.

One-on-one—A basic defensive position, whether at the attack position or the midfield.

1/6 principle—A rule stating approximately one goal will be scored for every six shots taken.

Outlet pass—A transition pass usually started by the goalie at the beginning of possession and of the clear.

Overload—Placing extra players on one side of the field, thus creating a difficult read for the defense.

Plane—Expressed as the "plane of the goal." An imaginary line running from the goal line to the restraining line. Also known as the "goal line extended."

Point—The position or area right behind the goal. Also known as X.

Point man (defense)—The defensive player on the fast break who is responsible for the fast-break middie.

Point man (offense)—The offensive player out front and on the side away from the fast-break middie.

Poke check—A defensive maneuver designated to dislodge the ball.

Power dodge—A natural move used to run past the opponent. Also known as the sweep and bull dodge.

Power phase—The initial movement of the stick. It is the time and distance the ball is in the stick.

Preparation phase—The initial phase, the starting position, of a shot or pass.

Prerotate—Sliding away from the man being covered and toward the next player.

Rake—A technique used on the face-off for controlling the ball. A sweeping motion of the stick in a particular direction. Also used as a technique to gain possession of the ball by placing the stick over the ball and pulling back, creating ball movement.

Red—Strictly a man-to-man call on defense. Also a "riding" call.

Regular—A term used in all phases of the game. For example, "regular offense," "regular defense," and "regular ride."

Reverse clamp—On the face-off, scooping the bottom part of the head of the stick under the opponent's stick and sweeping to the side.

Rifle technique—From a box position, taking the bottom hand and extending it to the side. This gives a quick checking move across the opponent's chest.

Roll dodge—A pivoting move in a circular motion, which is used to give the offensive player a position of advantage.

Rover—A specific player who is the backer on the rover defense, and the lone man on the gold defense.

Scooping—A technique used to gain possession of the ball while it is on the ground.

Shooters—An isolation offense supported by the three-man technique.

Shorty—The term used for the short-stick midfielders and where they are positioned.

Sideline—Designated midfield clear.

Single—The call made to riding close defender, informing how many players will move up to the midfield line when riding.

Sleeper—The defensive midfielder who stations himself at the midfield waiting for the five-man zone to get him the ball.

Slow break—The term used to describe a six-on-five, five-on-four, or six-on-four transition advantage.

Spike—Tells the half-field offense that one player, usually an attackman, will play directly on the crease. That player is responsible for the back door or backup on come-arounds.

Split dodge—Predominantly an open-field dodge with the offensive player running at a 45-degree angle and quickly bringing the stick across the body when he changes direction.

Spoke offense—An excellent control-type offense.

Spot shooting—Being aware as to where the ball should be shot in certain situations.

Squirm—The specific name given to the short-stick middie replacing the long-stick defender when clearing.

Stack—Diagonal two-man high-low post usually on both sides of the crease. Run out of a 1-4-1 formation usually.

Stick position—A good teaching method, used in the proper stick position, is to refer to the position of the stick as to the hands of a clock.

Stretch—Specific clear placing all defensive players and midfielders to the side of the field.

STX—Refers to the defensive midfield group.

Switch—A call made by the defense to alert players that they will be switching men and responsibilities.

Tandem—Two offensive players on the crease with one playing low to the side and the other playing diagonally high away from the other.

Tendencies—The basic physical behavior of the various positions.

Third man—Usually the player next to the adjacent man. Two away from the ball.

Thirty-three post—A clearing pattern used when the ball is brought in from the back line. 3-1-3 offensive clearing pattern.

Thirty-three tight—EMO formation.

Tough—A four-man defense assisted by two rovers. Great change-of-pace defense.

Triangle—Designated midfield clear.

Umbrella—Extra man defensive coverage vs. the three-three offensive set.

Weak-side coverage—A right-handed defender playing a left-handed attacker, or vice-versa, in close coverage, having the top hand of the stick at the offensive player's right shoulder area, and at the same time, the bottom hand is in the small of the back.

Wheel offense—Constant-movement offense with the intention of catching the defenders off guard.

Wrap check—A defensive maneuver where the stick is driven across the chest of the offensive player by swinging the bottom hand under the elbow of the top hand.

Index

About the Author

One of the winningest coaches in the history of college lacrosse, Carl Runk was the Towson Tigers' lacrosse coach for thirty-one years. With 262 career victories at Towson, he ranks seventh on the NCAA Division I list of all-time coaching victories. The Tigers' coach from 1968 to 1998, he led Towson to a record of 262–161 and a .619 winning percentage. Along the way, he led the Tigers to twenty-four winning seasons, thirteen NCAA Tournament berths, six East Coast Conference titles, and the 1974 NCAA College Division national championship.

The fifth head coach in the history of Tigers lacrosse, he guided the Tigers to seven consecutive NCAA College Division Tournament appearances from 1973 to 1979. In 1974, he coached Towson to the national championship with an 18–17 overtime victory against Hobart. As a result, he was named the USILA Coach of the Year in 1974.

Under his direction, the Tigers advanced to the NCAA Division I Tournament five times.

In 1991, he led the Tigers to an improbable run at the NCAA National Championship game, where they lost to North Carolina. Along the way, the eleventh-seeded Towson team beat Virginia, Princeton, and Maryland.

He is the only coach to lead his team to the national championship game at both the university division and college division levels.

In thirty-one seasons, he coached sixty-seven All-Americans and four National Players of the Year. In addition, five of his former players were members of Team USA for the World Games.

Honored as Towson University's Coach of the Year twice, he was selected to coach in the North-South Game three times. Carl was inducted into the

Regional Lacrosse Hall of Fame in 2000 and the Towson University Hall of Fame in 2007.

A native of Baltimore who attended Patterson High School, Coach Runk graduated from the University of Arizona in 1962. While coaching at Arizona, he posted a 28–4 record, which included an undefeated season, 11–0, and the Rocky Mountain Conference Championship in 1967.

He returned to the Baltimore area in 1967, becoming the Tigers' first-ever football coach and fifth lacrosse coach.

As the Tigers' first football coach, he guided the Tigers through their first seasons of competition from 1968 to 1971. After the 1971 season, he stepped down as football coach to concentrate on lacrosse.

Coach Runk has been a member of Towson University's Department of Kinesiology for forty years. He also initiated the sign language classes at the university and taught sign language for many years.

He and his wife, Joan, have four children and nine grandchildren.